Words: Beyond the Dictionary

A Philosophy and Random Thoughts

by

Ben R. Leonard, M.D.

authorHOUSE™

1663 LIBERTY DRIVE, SUITE 200
BLOOMINGTON, INDIANA 47403
(800) 839-8640
WWW.AUTHORHOUSE.COM

First published by AuthorHouse 09/10/04

ISBN: 1-4184-8681-7 (sc)

Printed in the United States of America
Bloomington, Indiana

This book is printed on acid-free paper.

Words: Beyond the Dictionary

Acknowledgements

I want to thank family & friends who read through my book looking for errors.

I particularly want to thank my daughter, Tina,

who did an excellent job of editing for me.

Words: Beyond the Dictionary

Dedications

This book is dedicated to my Wife who spent

lonely hours waiting as I wrote

and

To my Family and Friends

for their love and understanding.

Table of Contents

Introduction

This book of essays was started with the hope that it would allow my family and friends some insight into the way I think and feel. As it progressed, it became increasingly clear to me that I was philosophizing, advising, baring my spirit and soul, and in many instances, just ruminating and rambling. So one might say this is a multipurpose book – or a hodge-podge of opinions, philosophy, and advice. Just remember as you read that I do not claim to be erudite, wise, or invariably right.

I did not write this book to be a tome – I tried to keep each essay brief. I feel neither extremely intelligent nor knowledgeable. I do feel that I am thoughtful and honest in this presentation. You, the reader, may disagree with much of what I have to say, but give some of your own thought to it. In some small way, it may put you in better touch with yourself.

The format is simple. I requested family and friends to submit words to me, most of which I chose to use as well as some randomly picked words. I wrote an individual essay about the meaning of each word to me after first writing in and deliberating on a general dictionary definition of each word. Many words have multiple definitions, and I took the liberty of choosing the definitions that I wished to address.

There may be some who are offended by some of my ideas and thoughts. To you, I apologize and say that all I have written was with benign intent. I do not wish to proselytize. I am not so simple as to believe that we must agree or that I can or should try to change your way of feeling or thinking. Whether you agree with me entirely, only a bit, or not at all, please understand that my main concern is that you think. If I have stimulated thought, then my book is a success. If I have offered some useable advice, this enhances the success. If you come away from your reading with the feeling that my thoughts are honest and from the heart and without malice, this is my greatest reward. I hope you enjoy.

Ben R. Leonard, MD

November, 2003

Abortion

Dictionary Definition

"Abort: To bring forth premature or stillborn offspring; Give birth prematurely; To terminate pregnancy before term."

Beyond the Dictionary

Abortion is a frequent physiological occurrence when there is a significant pathological process either of the mother or the fetus; however, this is not the facet of fetal termination I wish to address.

First, let it be known that I am "Pro-choice" in the decision of all mothers to abort or not to abort. I must explain.

At this writing I have been in the practice of medicine for more than 50 years – years which have made me see a multitude of different situations. I think most agree that abortion is necessary when the life of the mother is at stake or the fetus is obviously so mal-formed that reasonable life would be impossible. The major disagreement comes when neither of these two situations exist.

I point out several hypothetical situations in which I feel the judgment to abort must be left to the mother:

> A teenage girl still in school who, if she has a child, will have a life of unfulfilled dreams, a life of resentment, and very likely a life of poverty.
>
> A young woman who has been or is on street drugs.
>
> A woman who is multigravida and already has a house over-run by children whom she can barely attend.
>
> Any woman who flatly states that she hates children.

None of these potential mothers would give a child the necessary love, concern, or attention so vital in raising a happy, productive human being. I have seen all too many devastated mothers and children living a life of pure hell – Life?

Is this life?

I've heard the arguments that these mothers brought it on themselves, but mistakes are made, and the child has no blame. Let's not damn these innocents to such misery.

Adventure

Dictionary Definition

"An undertaking involving danger and unknown risks; Exciting or remarkable experience."

Beyond the Dictionary

Adventure - The definition beautifully describes life which involves danger and unknown risks as well as exciting and remarkable experiences; however, this is a general description.

There are a plethora of adventures to be had by those who are inquisitive, vigorous, and possess the lust for life, the lust for freshness and excitement.

There is the adventure of travel, of sport, of learning, of teaching, of loving. There are so very many avenues to adventure. One does not have to sit idly by and allow adventure to flow from life - there is the option of seeking.

There are far away and near at hand places which offer excitement and beauty: Mountains, Lakes and Rivers, Oceans and Seas, Beautiful Forests and Valleys, Magnificent Cities and Charming Villages, all to be visited, enjoyed, and to satisfy our need for the unusual - our need for adventure.

There are sports aplenty to add that spice of adventure - too numerous to list.

Importantly, there are the wonderful adventures of teaching and learning. It is difficult to imagine a greater thrill than grasping new bits of knowledge or imparting that knowledge.

And the ultimate adventure is that of loving and being loved.

All kinds of love: the passionate and exciting love of romantic lovers, the warm and fulfilling love of friends, and the deep and abiding love of families. There is adventure in the broader love of our fellow human beings and for many the love of God or the

3

Ben R. Leonard, M.D.

contemplation of God. Sad, indeed, must be those who have not known love, the ultimate adventure.

Agnostic

Dictionary Definition

"One who holds that any ultimate reality, as God, is unknown and probably unknowable."

Beyond the Dictionary

Agnosticism makes more sense to me than atheism or than belief in a specific known God.

To address the first half of this argument, I must simply say that there appears to be some kind of thought and design to the universe and particularly our planetary system with the sun, moon, and stars. There certainly must be thoughtful design and higher planning to our earth and its multiple facets. So, from where does this marvelous creation arise? Just a simple "Big Bang" with no other explanation? OK, whence came the "Big Bang?" There had to be a creative power, or how did we evolve to the marvels of our present? Why not call that power God?

The second half of the argument is just as puzzling to me. For eons mankind has attempted to assign creation and the mysteries of life to one god or another or another or another. In ancient times the Greeks, Romans, Asians, Africans, etc. all had their gods. The native Americans had their gods. Later Judaism and Christianity developed. Today there are a myriad of religions in the world. Who was or is right? Or are they all wrong? I say that all religions and sects are man-made to suit the particular needs of the society in their particular time and place. One certainty is that each religion has followers who "KNOW" their religion is the true one; therefore, they believe all others are wrong.

OK, I think both arguments are wrong – I feel that atheism is too far one direction and distinct religions too far the other. I'm a fence straddler. I can't believe there is no creator, no God. I can't believe that so many divergent religions can all be right.

5

Ben R. Leonard, M.D.

Call me an agnostic, but please know that I really don't know who or what is right in this greatest of all mysteries.

Ambition

Dictionary Definition

"Ardent desire for rank, fame, or power; Desire to achieve a particular end; Strong desire for advancement or success."

Beyond the Dictionary

Generally, ambition is a good thing leading to successful careers, productive lives, and acceptable or exceptional wealth, but more importantly the results of ambition often allow for exceptional service.

Certainly, I do not downplay the personal benefits of ambition. It is a wonderful thing to afford a nice home, good food and clothing, travel and entertainment, and a good education for one's family. I think most would agree with this; however, as I grow older, I recognize an equally valuable asset the ambitious, therefore successful, person attains: the asset of being able to help.

How marvelous it is to have attained sufficient success to be able to direct some of that ambitious energy to the benefit of other less fortunate members of the human race or the animal kingdom.

Many of our wealthiest individuals become our greatest philanthropists, establish wonderful charities and foundations, and even serve actively in these endeavors. Many of lesser monetary wealth, but still ambitious, work and give of their time and money toward the betterment of people and animals.

It is easy to give lip service to charity and philanthropic endeavors, but it takes ambition and effort to be effective in them.

There is a flip side to ambition. I shall give this only scant attention. Simply consider a short list of some ambitious people:

Ben R. Leonard, M.D.

Hitler, Stalin, Hussein, Bin Laden, many Roman Emperors and many dictators, and more. Need I say more in this regard?

When morally directed, ambition is a good thing. On balance, there seems to be more good than bad from this trait, ambition.

Anger

Dictionary Definition

"Strong feeling of displeasure and usually of antagonism; Emotional excitement induced by intense displeasure."

Beyond the Dictionary

In fact, why in the world should we ever become angry when we consider the consequences?

Anger distorts our ability to think clearly, our ability to reason, and often it causes us to act in harmful ways and in ways we, more often than not, regret. Yet it is often so powerfully induced that we seem unable to combat the emotion. There are those who find it so difficult to avoid becoming angry that they actually must seek professional "anger control." We have all known people who destroy property, who cause bodily harm to themselves and others, and who wreak emotional havoc due to an angry response to a stimulus which could easily have been resolved with a calm, reasoned response.

Lucky are those individuals who are able to control their emotions. They ultimately are more productive and happier people, and they are far more pleasant and easier to be around and to deal with. I'm guessing, but I would be willing to bet that those with a more even temperament tend to be more successful in all of life's endeavors. They are able to approach all situations more thoughtfully and rationally. This does not mean they are unemotional. In fact they are better able to develop the good emotions, the productive emotions. They have the emotional strength to drive, to sustain, to succeed.

Having said all that, I must admit I still "get mad." I'm not one of the lucky ones, but I recognize there is a way to control anger with preemptive thought and deliberation, and I am trying, with some success, to use this tool.

My advice: Parents, Be good role models and teachers, and in being and teaching you will be a double success. All adults, be thoughtful and deliberate, and you'll ultimately gain control of your anger and be happier and more productive."

Arms

Dictionary Definition

"Means of offense or defense."

Beyond the Dictionary

The subject of this essay is not about a part of the human body, but about weapons.

What do you suppose God was thinking when he gave humans the traits of avarice, jealousy, lust, immorality, and evilness? Then to top it off, he bestowed us the emotions of anger and hate with the added spice of the love of killing. So with all of these delightful tid-bits roiling in our brains, it was only natural that we arm ourselves to defend or offend or simply hunt.

Stones, knives, spears, bows & arrows, then guns! The earliest homosapiens to our more recent ancestors required these implements to hunt for food to survive and, of course, to defend.

Too bad, but we must forgive them. They hunted and fought for survival.

Today, guns are used for hunting, but we no longer need to hunt for food; rather we hunt for pleasure – for the joy of killing. What a wonderful pleasure it must be to kill and maim the birds in our sky and the animals of our forest. Certainly, they feel no pain!!!! My heart cries for them!!!!

Even more marvelous is our addition of bombs and other charming Weapons of Mass Destruction to our arsenal of delightful delicacies. What in God's name are we doing? We are supposed to be creatures of conscience.

Only recently the President of the United States approved the production of MOAB, Massive Ordnance Air Burst, a 22,000-pound bomb that has massive killing and destructive power sending a cloud of smoke and debris 20,000 feet into our atmosphere. And we have a supply of atomic weapons adequate to destroy the earth!

Don't we have a charming and delightful world? What a beautiful legacy we leave our children.

Atheist

Dictionary Definition

"One who denies existence of God."

Beyond the Dictionary

I think perhaps those who call themselves atheists actually are pretty good observers of humanity and certainly must have given thought to the diverse religions that have been devised by humankind.

It seems evident that such a diverse array of gods that have been worshiped by so many diverse societies simply can't all be existent; therefore, it rather easily follows that there is no true god. Hence, there should be no theism.

I recognize the partial truth in this rationale. I too feel that the multiple religious beliefs tend to cancel one another out, but I find it difficult to rule out God. I do not find it difficult to rule out multiple gods, nor do I find it difficult to reject the god of each specific religion.

I have contended over and over again that there is a creative power with the ability to think, to plan, to organize, and to effectuate. This is the creator of all things both earthly and ethereal, both human and spiritual. Why not call our creator God?

This rationale brings me to refute atheism as we customarily consider it – the absolute rejection of the concept of God. On the other hand, if we consider atheism as the refusal to worship God, there appears to be a more rational argument. From this viewpoint, there is acknowledgement that the concept of god is possible, but that worship of God from a theistic standpoint is unacceptable. Perhaps this philosophical position is correct. Who knows? Certainly no one, to my belief, has really talked to God to find out if worship is expected or mandatory. And God, as the creator of "ALL," has not created a perfect world free of terror, violence, and pain. Is one expected to worship a God who has created such a world? I don't know – I'm human, and I just don't know. But I know I believe in God – I can't be an atheist.

Books

Dictionary Definition

Book: "A set of written sheets of skin or paper or tablets of wood or ivory; A set of written, printed, or blank sheets bound together in a volume; Long written or printed literary composition."

Beyond the Dictionary

The definition is pretty dry for something so wonderful. Just stop to consider. Where would you be, what would life be like without books?

The history of writing and printing is fascinating. Clay tablets from before 3,000 BC show a kind of script recording the affairs of the Babylonians. The invention of writing is credited to the ancient Mesopotamians where Iraq now stands. Then we take a quick hop to 1452 when Gutenberg put together the printing press. Voila! Books! How's that for a quick history lesson?

So much of what we teach and learn is found in books. Reading is the basis of education, and books are where we must and most frequently go to read to learn. Once we have mastered the art of reading, the world opens up to us. We obtain knowledge; we strengthen our ability to think; we become better able to be gainfully employed; and yes, we even find another wondrous highway to adventure, excitement, and pleasure. Books are Brain Food! Books are Fun Food!

Think of the impact various books have had on society. Lives have been changed by the Bible and the Koran. Lives have been destroyed by the plan of Hitler's Mein Kampf. Mark Twain gave us wonderful adventures in our youth. What child hasn't delighted in those inimitable Dr. Seuss books? The list goes on and on. Perhaps we didn't enjoy every thing we had to read in our school days, but as we look back, just consider the fantastic array of facts in our history books, our geography books, our political science books, our philosophy books, our science and math books, our psychology books, our business books, etc, etc.

My heart goes out to those who never learn to read. They miss so very much.

Brave

Dictionary Definition

"Having courage." [Courage: "Mental or moral strength to venture, persevere, and withstand danger,or fear."]

Beyond the Dictionary

What a wonderful thing it is to be brave. There are so many instances in life requiring bravery, and if we meet them with bravery, we end up winning the game of life. Bravery allows us dignity, self-respect, and the respect of others.

There are many types of bravery brought on by multiple situations: the bravery required of those in mortal battle, the bravery required of a dying person, the bravery required of one watching a loved one die, the bravery to face one in power, the bravery to stand for what one feels is right.

All too frequently there are those who must face several or more of these situations. If they buckle under, they lose so very much. If they stand up and fight, they win so very much!

How does one become brave? First, it is probably necessary to have the feeling of being right. Second, one must learn to control fear – not an easy job, but imperative. Third, one must have moral strength and mental resolve. Surprisingly, there are a great many brave people on this earth, and we can thank The Almighty that we have a super abundance of such people in these United States of America.

We've been taught well that our country stands for that which is right. Most of our parents and teachers have imparted this sense to our youth as well as stressing the importance of facing adversity with courage. Unhappily, I detect a trend away from these values. Perhaps this is because many of our citizens are members of sects or religions which are not endemic to America.

Ben R. Leonard, M.D.

Perhaps the increasing number of inordinately young parents or single parents has a deleterious affect on our youth. Perhaps our political leaders have let us down. Actually, these are questions, not answers.

In any event we should all try to teach our youth the values and traits required to be brave.

Charity

Dictionary Definition

"Benevolent goodwill toward or love of humanity; Kindly liberality and helpfulness esp. toward the needy or suffering; Aid given those in need; A gift for public benevolent purposes."

Beyond the Dictionary

Food for the hungry, shelter and bed for the homeless, relief for the pained, comfort for the dying, solace for the distressed – What noble and necessary gifts these are. They not only serve a need, but they also lift the human spirit.

So frequently we hear the word "Compassion" bantered about. I sometimes feel offended at the light & easy use of such an important word – without compassion there can be no charity. In fact the two driving forces of charity are love and compassion for all things great & small, animal or human, all the things that nature and man have wrought. Charity is not to be given or taken lightly – Freely, yes; lightly, no.

Charity should be left out of the political arena. It cannot be classified Liberal or Conservative, Republican or Democratic, Green or Libertarian. It must be the shared purview of all.

There will always be those less fortunate in our world – sometimes of their own making, sometimes through unavoidable misfortune. I have heard the argument that each individual is responsible for his or her own circumstances. I can agree with this only with regard to those who are indolent and unwilling to work, but we must remember there are those who, through no fault of their own, are injured, mentally retarded, hungry, or poor. They need charity.

How sad for those who lack charitableness – for those whose greed, avarice, or hate will not allow them to give. They will never feel the beautiful, heady feeling of helping.

Ben R. Leonard, M.D.

Happily, charitable is easy to be; charity is easy to give, and the feeling that charity endows both to the giver and the recipient is far more valuable than the gift itself. Charity does, indeed, transcend mere humanity – It lifts the human spirit into the sky.

Children

Dictionary Definition

Child: "Young person especially between infancy and youth."

Beyond the Dictionary

What can I say about children that hasn't been said thousands of times? They are a blessing. They are cute, funny, and adorable. They are a pain in the ass. They are the future. It's all been said, and it's all true.

Children are little sponges that soak up experiences and education at an unbelievably rapid rate. It is almost inconceivable that from birth to age 18 they learn to talk, to read, to write, to sing, to dance, to play, and so much more. They learn to plan, to think, and to dream of a future. What a miracle of learning!

They begin their existence so innocent and benign. Their only needs are a full tummy and a clean diaper. Then they start the maturation process watching and imitating their elders. They are taught an array of rights and wrongs. They are taught kindness or cruelty, love or hate, charity or avarice, morality or immorality, honesty or dishonesty, and sometimes a mixture of all these.

Sooner or later they are brought to the realization that few things are free and that most wants and needs must be the provision of work. Those who learn and accept this at a reasonably early age seem to be the ones who mature the most rapidly. They seem to be the ones who accept education as a vital part of their life.

In the teen years, their emotions begin to mature and their hormones begin to rage. This a time for more learning and a time for them to exercise the "rights and wrongs" they have been taught. This a time when parental influence and control begin to wane. Parents, cross your fingers!

Ben R. Leonard, M.D.

The lucky children are those who have been loved, nurtured, cherished, and correctly taught. They will be the good citizens, the doers, the givers, and the teachers.

Complacent

Dictionary Definition

"Self-satisfied; Marked by inclination to please or oblige; Unconcerned."

Beyond the Dictionary

Complacency is not a bad trait to have unless you have an important and demanding job to do in which case it is potentially devastating. Truly complacent people seldom achieve the goals of pleasing or obliging. The unconcerned attitude of the complacent causes them to be unfulfilling – jobs and projects end up undone or late. Unhappily, for those who depend upon such individuals often find they have been disappointed and often damaged in some way.

On the other hand, complacent people tend to be more content than the driving, intent types, and contentment is a form of happiness.

I honestly have trouble judging which type of person is the happier. Certainly, it is nice to be complacent and content, but there is happiness and satisfaction in the achievement of the more ambitious and vigorous people.

The old cliché, "It takes all kinds," is most assuredly true, and I have no strong feelings one way or the other thinking that each individual should be judged as such. There are good and bad complacent folks, and there are good and bad in the opposite character class.

All of the above being noted, I would rather associate with the driving, vigorous, ambitious people, and I prefer to think that I am one of them. I prefer the exciting aspects of life rather than what I consider the dull and more laid back.

Most importantly, regardless of your character traits, cause no harm.

To each his own. To each her own.

Conscience

Dictionary Definition

"Sense or consciousness of the moral goodness or blameworthiness of one's own conduct, intentions, or character together with feeling of obligation to do right or be good; A faculty, power, or principle enjoining good acts; Sensitive regard for fairness or justice."

Beyond the Dictionary

What a wonderful world it would be if we all had a good functioning conscience, but it just ain't so!

Consciences come in a multitude of sizes and shapes. The variations can't all be right, but show me the person who feels that he or she has a bad conscience. Most people justify their acts in their mind in some way, be the acts good or bad.

Yet one wonders about the thieves, rapists, terrorists, abusers, and murderers. What goes on in their minds? How do they justify their acts? Do they have a conscience? If not, why not?

Maybe some consciences are bad, and there is a flaw in the definition of the word. Some people seem to have no regard for right or wrong, for fairness or justice. I would be so bold as to presume that a bad conscience is just one of the varieties of sizes and shapes.

What's the cause of this variety in consciences? There is not a bit of science involved in the conclusion I have drawn – it's pure gut feeling. I feel there is little gene linkage in the development of our conscience. I am more inclined to feel that the etiology of each particular conscience is psychosocial. It is a product of our family training, our social environment, and our educational environment. If we are abused by those we are supposed to respect and obey, if we see them violating the law; then we are apt to develop a conscience which allows this type of activity. If, on the other hand, our parents and mentors are kind and law abiding, we are more apt to develop a good conscience.

I wish each of you a good conscience and a better world.

Contraception

Dictionary Definition

"Intentional prevention of conception or impregnation."

Beyond the Dictionary

Contraception? Why? Let's just consider a few figures obtained from the U.S. Census Bureau as of today, November 23, 2003.

World population in 1950 was 2,555,360,972. World population estimated as of today by World POPClock Projection is 6,331,711,291. This represents an increase of almost four trillion people in just 53 years! Further World POPClock Projection estimates our earth will have 9,084,495,405 people in the year 2050. These numbers are so tremendous that they defy our imagination. Remember, Planet Earth is not growing, and it is crowded to the hilt with human beings now. How will it support over 2.5 trillion more bodies 47 years from now? I worry about my children and grandchildren.

I recognize there are those who are constrained by religion to use contraception, but I doubt that they have truly considered the effects of their abundant procreation on future generations or for that matter on the present generation. In my practice of family medicine I attend numerous families with 3, 4, 5, 6, or more children. I ask myself how can they adequately feed, clothe, and house all of these little ones soon to be teen-agers wanting an education. Then they become young adults needing employment. How do they survive with at least a modicum of life's necessities much less a few niceties? As each year goes by, the competition for jobs will increase, and the welfare roles will likewise increase.

I haven't even touched on the unwanted pregnancies of young mothers [and fathers] not yet ready for the responsibilities of parenting. These are children having children about to have their lives turned upside down or possibly destroyed. The added harm of such pregnancies is that done to the offspring. Often they

Ben R. Leonard, M.D.

are neglected and/or mistreated and grow into psychologically damaged, unhappy adults.

Contraception. Wrong or immoral? Baloney! We'd better start using it, or we're in trouble. And it beats the hell out of abortion!

Cowardly

Dictionary Definition

Coward — "One who shows shameful fear or timidity."

Beyond the Dictionary

If we consider what being cowardly is in its full meaning, we must admit that it is a dishonorable trait. It means that fear has conquered. Subjugation to fear is more often than not the thief of reason and the road to failure and dishonor.

It is not a bad thing to feel frightened; indeed, fear is most often a good thing. It gives us pause to think, reason, and plan. It prevents us from blindly rushing into dangerous and often catastrophic situations. But, unless we succumb to fear in a cowardly way and retreat, we analyze those situations, and we handle them as bravely and with as much reason as time and particular circumstances will allow.

Judgment is not always easy. Often there is little or no time for thought or reason. In such cases your emotions or subconscious will drive your action. These are the times when love or hate or need motivate. These are transcendental moments - times that often separate the brave from the cowardly.

However, at times it is not cowardly to back away from danger; it is only cowardly when the danger is of extreme importance.

Frightening situations must be approached with thought and reason if possible. There are times when retreat is appropriate and certainly not dishonorable. Why rush into the jaws of a lion or stand in the path of a bullet unless it is to save those who may be more dear to you than life? You are not a coward if you turn away from a useless battle.

Courage and cowardice are easy to talk about, but in the final analysis only living your life will finally decide which will describe you. My wish for all is that you are never cowardly and that you find strength and courage when the cause is right. It is my hope that you encounter little to fear in your life.

Be brave, but think when thought is possible.

Cremation

Dictionary Definition

Cremate – "Reduce to ashes by burning."

Beyond the Dictionary

I recognize there are those who abhor the thought of cremation, or probably more specifically of being cremated – some for religious reasons, some due to fear of the unknown. Personally, I have no such feelings, and in fact, I strongly support the act of cremation.

I'm sure most of the readers are familiar with the theory that our bodies serve merely as the vessels of our true selves, of our souls. I subscribe to this theory and have no compunction about my mortal body being converted into ashes. I have no idea what will happen to my soul, but I doubt that the flames will touch it.

Why not bury our human remains without conflagration as most do? The answer is over-population and lack of space. It's pure and simple; our world is finite in its space and our population is infinitely expanding. All too rapidly we will run out of places to inter our dead. Cremation seems to be part of the answer. Contraception and population control are other avenues we should more aggressively pursue but do not preclude the need for cremation.

For those who object to cremation for religious reasons, I would urge you to reconsider your position in light of saving space for your progeny and other future humans. What more can I say?

For those who fear cremation, I'm willing to bet we won't feel a thing. Of course, no one has ever come back to let us know, but I bet I'm right.

Cry

Dictionary Definition

"Inarticulate utterance of distress, rage, or pain; Weep, sob."

Beyond the Dictionary

Lives there a person with soul so dead who has not wept?

Recognizing the multiple uses and meanings of the word "cry," I wish to address only the meaning as it applies to the shedding of tears.

Do you cry? I cry!

As toddlers, little boys are taught that it is not manly to cry. How thoughtless this notion is and really how unfeeling. When we are physically or mentally hurt, one of the first impulses is to cry. When we see or hear of others grievously injured, we cry.

When we remember sad events, we cry. We even cry for happiness.

Crying is a natural phenomenon. Crying is an emotional outlet that allows us to heal more easily or to celebrate more meaningfully. Crying is mental and emotional catharsis. If we contain our tears, we also contain our pain and sorrow, and at times, we don't fully express our joy. Without tears we tend to box in our emotions and allow them to stunt our humanity.

As I have grown older, I find that my tears come more easily. Sometimes it takes only a sad or a fond memory, a moving speech or song, a lovely view, or the site of one I love to bring me to tears. I often try to hide these tears since I'm a man, and was trained as a boy that crying is for girls. Ha! How stupid!

I'm a human being, and I cry. If I'm hurt, I cry. If I'm happy, I cry. If I'm sad, I cry. So, you he-men, put that in your pipe, and smoke it!

Ben R. Leonard, M.D.

I feel sorry for those unfortunate people who can't cry. Either they have a life so poor in events and people that they have nothing to cry about, or they have a soul so dead.

Cry a bit! You'll feel better!

Death

Dictionary Definition

"Permanent cessation of all vital functions: the end of life."

Beyond the Dictionary

"A permanent cessation of all vital functions" – One wonders?

Perhaps it depends on the definition of "vital functions." Commonly we think of vital functions as eating, breathing, etc.; however, this excludes the "transcendental vital functions." The $64,000 question is what happens to the soul – does the soul permanently cease, or does it go on into a superhuman arena?

OK, so I'm being a bit esoteric or beyond, but who among us humans truly has the answer?

Oh, well, we all die, and we should not fear death. I understand that it represents the unknown to most of us, and there is uneasiness when we approach the unknown, but inevitability must supersede fear. We cannot rationally fight what is! Fear only distracts and distorts the final days of our earthly existence. Some way we should all try to face the inevitable with a calm resolution that we must and will take what comes.

There are two avenues to this attitude: religious and philosophical.

I personally prefer the philosophical approach with full recognition of God's power but without the faintest idea what God has in store for my soul. I simply cannot grasp the concept of Heaven or Hell or the other religions' hereafters. There are so many religions with various conceptions. How does one choose?

How can they all be right? How can they all be God inspired?

Never-the-less, those who approach death with religious faith are not wrong. Their belief gives them comfort and strength to die with dignity and without fear. In some ways I envy them, and they may be right.

Whatever one's approach to death, it should be done with sincerity, resolution, and dignity in the knowledge that it must be - there is no way to turn back nor should there be.

Divorce

Dictionary Definition

"Legal dissolution of a marriage."

Beyond the Dictionary

This word bothers me – it points up my failures, and this is uncomfortable.

Why are so many of us so careless in our thinking and planning? Why do we jump into commitments that clearly are a mistake? In a very troubling way, divorce is the breaking of a promise. What is the root of this instability that causes two people to lose love and forsake commitment?

If I could answer these questions, I would not be sitting here 3 times divorced. I married good women all of whom I still like, but some psychological phenomenon caused one of them to leave me and me to leave two of them. I still don't completely understand what happened, but I do have a deep sense of blame and shame.

I do not like divorce! I condone divorce as a necessary evil! I know that humans make mistakes, errors in judgment, which require correction, and often divorce is the only recourse.

There is a 50% divorce rate in the United States today. In my days of divorce, I represented an aberrant fraction. Today I'm a normal statistic. What a shame that people are, as a rule rather than as an exception, using my lack of good judgment in choosing and keeping a marriage partner.

What a shame it is to tear children from one parent or the other, to create single parent homes, to create financial havoc, and to present this instability to the family unit frequently only to find that one's situation is actually worsened.

I'm no sage, and I really have no answers, but I do advise young people to be very deliberate and thoughtful in choosing a marital partner, to carefully inspect their inner thoughts and emotions and desires, and once married, to work at keeping stable and happy – turn back only after deep deliberation.

Drug

Dictionary Definition

"Substance used as a medication or in the preparation of medication; A substance intended for use in diagnosis, cure, mitigation, treatment, or prevention of disease; A substance other than food intended to affect the structure or function of the body; A substance that causes addiction or habituation."

Beyond the Dictionary

Drugs have played, do play, and will continue to play an extremely important role in society as a whole and in individual lives - good and bad!

Human kinds' discovery that various substances have the power to mitigate and heal many of our infirmities is one of the world's greatest gifts. Daily, hourly, new drugs are being developed to enhance the field of medicine - drugs that can be used in virtually every medical specialty for almost every disease condition. How remarkable and wonderful!

Yet there is the flip side of the coin. There are three areas of concern, and they all relate to the mis-use of drugs: prescription drug side effects, so called over-the-counter drugs, and illegal street drugs.

Prescription drugs are legal and generally very helpful. The concern in their use is perhaps three-fold: allergic reactions, harmful side effects, and faulty prescribing habits by physicians. All of these can be fairly well handled by concerned & ethical physicians. Many physicians seem insulted when patients, usually computer buffs, point out side effect profiles to them, but I consider this to be a good thing. There is such an abundance of drugs on the market today that it is impossible for any doctor to know all of the details of each one. It is good for the patient to be aware.

Legal over-the-counter preparations can be helpful, but the same constraints of allergy and harmful side effects apply. It is strongly advisable to thoroughly evaluate any drug before using. Your doctor's office is a good place to start. It should be axiomatic that no person takes any drug without knowledge of the potential harm.

Illegal street drugs! What can I say? They destroy lives and families. How stupid and thoughtless it is for anyone to use them. Their control seems beyond the government. Of course, we should continue to apprehend and convict dealers, but the final answer lies with the users. With every fiber of their bodies they must try to stop, and our youth must be educated to desist.

I realize these comments are like whistling in a gale, but if we all whistle, perhaps we'll be heard.

Dying

Dictionary Definition

"Pres part. of die." Die: "To pass from physical life."

Beyond the Dictionary

The act of dying is far different, and at least from a temporal standpoint, far more important than death itself. From the moment we are born until the day we actually die, we are in the act of dying. In our childhood and youth and even our mid-life, we give this little or no thought. In fact we feel immortal. This is as it should be. The thought or thinking of dying should be left to the elderly.

Unhappily, there are all too many of the young who must face death. I address this briefly with full knowledge of the sad and devastating nature of young death. My heart bleeds for the young people who must die in battle. I grieve for the little ones who die of serious disease or starvation or abuse. I can only hope and wish that there is some relieving factor in their ending.

Most who die are old, those who have lived a full life, and must make way for the young. And death for the elderly is really not so bad. As we go through life, we gather experience, hopefully some wisdom, and a philosophical attitude – and we get a little tired. We know death awaits us; we know it is inevitable, and if we really think about it, we don't fear it. In fact we look on it as a good and proper thing – the way to get a good, and hopefully, well deserved rest.

Certainly, each person faces dying in his or her own particular way according to the dictates of philosophy or religion, but common to all is, or should be, acceptance. Hopefully, this acceptance is well sugar-coated with the knowledge that life has been full and well run and that for that life the world is a better place – doesn't have to be a lot better place; a fraction better will do.

Ben R. Leonard, M.D.

If we have the inner peace that we have left a loving family and friends with good memories, the way to good lives, and love and happiness, then dying and death have no sting.

Education

Dictionary Definition

Educate: "To develop mentally or morally esp. by instruction."

Beyond the Dictionary

It's a wonderful thing to educate and to become educated – `wonderful for the teacher and wonderful for the student. The primary thrust of this essay is directed toward the student, yet in no way to diminish the important roles of teacher and mentor.

I simply cannot over emphasize the importance of education and the several very important ways it adds to one's life. First, and most obviously, education adds to knowledge, and who would deny the benefits of knowledge? Second, education improves our ability to comprehend and think. Third, it enhances our ability to enjoy – our joie de vivre. Fourth, and many would say least important, it lends to our position or prestige.

That education is one of the chief routes to knowledge is commonly accepted, and knowledge is one of life's most important tools. Added to the ability to think and comprehend, which education improves, knowledge gives us the power to advance our lot in life and to add to the benefit of society.

Ah, Joie de vivre! The joy of life and living! The world is jam-packed with pleasures: Music, Art, Literature, Theater, Sports, Dance, ad infinitum. All of these can be enjoyed by most, but the greater enjoyment goes to those who have the greatest comprehension and knowledge of what they are enjoying. And comprehension and knowledge are, in great part, products of education.

Many would contend that position and prestige are not very important. I agree to a degree. It is more important to be a good and giving person. This applies to all humans. The caveat applies to those of a bit more intelligence who have the need to reach a higher status. These are the people who need a degree in higher education to reach positions of leadership. In any event, education is a very important element in life. Get one!

Evil

Dictionary Definition

"Morally reprehensible; Sinful; Wicked; Something that brings sadness, distress, or calamity."

Beyond the Dictionary

Ask anyone: "Are you evil?" What answer would you expect and, 99.9999% of the time, receive? No! Of course not!

Presuming true the concept that no one wishes to be thought of as evil, why do we see and experience so much evil in the world? Perhaps those who are evil simply do not know what is and is not evil – there is a blank area in their super-ego. They somehow become unaware of the rules of society and lose, or never gain, the moral attitudes, conscience, and sense of guilt that are ingrained in most of us. Is this a product of their upbringing, of their early training? Surely there is no gene of evil.

What are the factors that produce the Hitlers, Husseins, Bin Ladens, Stalins, Attilas, et al? Who were their parents and mentors? What were the circumstances in their upbringing? Were they abused? What? What? What? I contend that if one is brought up mean, then one becomes mean. If one is brought up without a conscience, then one has no conscience. These are the people who abuse and vilify others to gratify their own greed and hate, and they don't realize their evilness.

Why are we so aware of evil? If I may be allowed to speculate, evil is so demanding on and fascinating to us that we insist our media inform of every instance of evil doing. It seems to me that we see and hear much more of evil via the media than we see and hear of goodness. I'm convinced this is not a good thing for society, but the reality is we want the bad news even though most of us are basically kind and good.

The heartening fact is most humans are basically good. We may not completely understand evil, but we recognize it, and we

Ben R. Leonard, M.D.

are willing to combat it. Evil will continue to raise its ugly head, but we will continue to chop away at it! AND HOORAY FOR US!

Exaggerate

Dictionary Definition

"To enlarge beyond bounds or veracity; To make an overstatement."

Beyond the Dictionary

Aw, shucks! Why not push the truth a bit at times? If it does no harm, play with the facts a little. Add a little spice to life.

I presume you understand my position on exaggeration, but I must clarify. I believe in moderation in most everything; not that I have always practiced what I preach. If not carried to extreme and if not persistent, exaggeration can be a good thing or a fun thing.

Consider the fisherman who didn't catch a fish. Why not let him say he caught a 20 pound bass? That's fun! Where's the harm?

Consider the hiker who walked a mile, but made it 20. That's fun! Where's the harm? Consider the golfer who shot 120, but said it was 80. That's fun! Where's the harm? That's the Walter Mitty in us coming to the surface with no harm intended or done.

All that being said, I certainly recognize the bad side of exaggeration. Reputations can be destroyed, friendships damaged, and love demolished with exaggerated stories and claims. These embellished tales are all too frequent in occurrence. Sometimes they are told with malicious intent, and their ill- purpose is served. There are even times when harmful stories are exaggerated with no ill intent. In either case, there is only harm done.

The moral of this argument is to keep your embellished stories benign in intent and thoughtful as to content. If you are a raconteur, think and be kind.

Have fun with your words!

Do no harm with your words!

Experience

Dictionary Definition

"Facts or events or the totality of facts or events observed; Knowledge, skill, or practice derived from direct observation or participation in events."

Beyond the Dictionary

Experience and formal education are the bases of knowledge and wisdom, and for good measure we must include skill.

It is wonderful and almost a necessity to have a formal education, but of equal importance is experience. We learn to learn in school. We further learn in living. In all the activities of life we gain experience.

Experience is the basis of good people and marital relations, good job skills, good recreational skills, and finally, along with knowledge, the basis of wisdom.

This does not mean that the young and inexperienced are incapable, therefore, unemployable. All it means is that they need to work in order to gain experience and to finally take the place of the their experienced elders. With experienced people the work world thrives and survives.

Just as important is experience in dealing with others. We learn from infancy that if we strike another, we are apt to be hit back and that if we take from another, we are likely to be punished; or if we offend another, there is often a sad price to pay. By experience we learn to be better people, better friends, better family members.

The greatest number of divorces occurs in the first few years of marriage. Why? Not enough experience! We need time to learn the art of living together as a marital team. The longer we live in a marriage, the greater the experience and the greater the chance for its survival.

Ben R. Leonard, M.D.

Pure old book learnin' and plenty of experience are the ingredients of wisdom. Not a guarantee, but the only way for the lucky few who finally become wise.

Faith

Dictionary Definition

"Belief and trust in and loyalty to a God; Belief in the traditional doctrines of a religion; Firm belief in something for which there is no proof."

Beyond the Dictionary

I personally have difficulty with the perceived notion of faith because, to me, it implies complete trust to the point of "personally knowing" that certain doctrines or certain specific gods or icons are representative of absolute truth. Again and again I ask myself how so many different belief systems or religions or sects, all having divergent and completely different doctrines, can be absolutely right. Each one claims to be the ultimate truth; each one claims to be faultless, and each one demands total acceptance - total faith. How can so many be totally right leaving so many totally wrong? As much as I would love to know the "Ultimate Truth," I feel that it has not been sufficiently proven to me, and I must, in honesty, remain in the limbo of having faith in a God instead of the God of a specific religion. Well, I guess in the final analysis I do have a certain type of faith.

We commonly attach the notion of faith to God and religion which is what I discussed above, but there are other connotations. I particularly refer to the faith we have in certain people and the good faith we so often display in dealing with our friends, family, and jobs.

We all have friends and family members in whom we place our complete faith and trust. We know that when they promise us something or when we need something, it will be done. A great many people can be depended upon to carry out job and life assignments in good faith - they are honest, dependable, and faithful.

Ben R. Leonard, M.D.

When one stops to consider, being faithful and having faith are wonderful attributes. It makes your life more admired by others and gives you great self-esteem. And to have faith in God, no matter which God, can impart a beautiful peace of mind.

I must admit I'm a little shaky in the religious faith department.

Family

Dictionary Definition

"A group of persons of common ancestry; The basic unit in society having as a nucleus two or more adults living together and cooperating in the care and rearing of their own or adopted children; A people or group of peoples regarded as deriving from a common stock."

Beyond the Dictionary

People need people, and even the poorest among us have this need filled with family. One of nature's greatest gifts to most humans is family united by the common bond of blood.

We share the good and the bad times with family. Holidays, those happy days of celebration, are shared by family members; births and birthdays are family events; moments of good fortune are cause for family rejoicing. By the same token, family members gather to protect one another; they hasten to assist one another in hard times; they lend love and support in times of sickness. These are the lovely and wonderful things that most often occur with families.

Yet, unhappily, there are dysfunctional families – those with deserting members, those with cruel or sadistic members, those with immoral members, those with indolent members, those with dishonest members, and even those with members incapable of love. It is difficult for me, as I am sure it is for most, to imagine being a part of a stressed, dysfunctional family, but such families do exist.

These unhappy, often turbulent, families are the chief producers of our criminal element and of many of our psychopathic and sociopathic personalities. Think of the millions of dollars these people cost us and the danger to which they expose us! What can be done? Perhaps a small part of the answer lies with our schools and teachers, but this is basically not their responsibility.

Ben R. Leonard, M.D.

To be honest, I have no answer. Perhaps wiser heads than mine can supply the answers we need.

I give daily thanks that my, and most, families are wonderful, loving, and successful – that they fulfill life's good purposes.

Fanatic

Dictionary Definition

"Marked by excessive enthusiasm and intense uncritical devotion."

Beyond the Dictionary

How very stupid is the fanatic! To follow a leader or an idea or ideal, no matter how evil or good, without question or inspection is indeed stupid, and to do so with unbridled enthusiasm is twice stupid.

Certainly fanatics can do tremendous good, but the same good can be accomplished with rational thought and deliberate action, often with a more lasting effect.

What concern me more are the fanatics of evil. These are the people who, with little or no thought to their own safety, plunder, burn, bomb, murder, and terrorize.

Most often they carry out their heinous acts in the name of their god or a political cause little realizing that such fanaticism causes more hostile reaction and resultant harm to their cause than reasonable argument and diplomatic negotiation.

The fact is normal people are frightened of such intense devotion and action - frightened even of the good deeds done with undue and excessive enthusiasm. This fear often, probably more often than not, leads to dislike and even hate.

It's too bad and frequently tragic that those fanatic personalities fail to realize the double harm they cause - the harm they do others and the harm they do themselves and their beliefs. What causes this gross obtuseness, this insensitivity?

The fanatic personality must be a product of youthful training. There is inherent in all humans the need to survive. Somehow this is trained out of the fanatic - perhaps brainwashed is better terminology. Such irrational fervor has to be the product of brainwashing!

We must all give thanks that there are more of us than of them.

Fear

Dictionary Definition

"A disagreeable, often strong, emotion caused by anticipation or awareness of danger."

Beyond the Dictionary

Fear is not a really bad emotion and certainly not to be avoided.

It is one of our most important warning systems.

Fear is at least uncomfortable and at worst horrifying and terrible; therefore, it seems to be the general consensus that fear is a bad thing and hopefully to be avoided. If this be the case, how do we teach our children, and how do we avoid danger? Indeed, how do we survive?

We teach our children to stay out of the streets, to avoid unknown waters, to stay away from strangers, and to avoid multiple other dangerous situations. Of course, this is thoughtful and reasonable, but the basic motivating emotion is fear. We just don't usually think of fear as being such a useful tool.

In a certain sense fear is the reason we do almost everything in life. We educate because we fear being unemployable; we work because we fear poverty; we eat and take vitamin supplements because we fear illness; we marry because we fear loneliness and the lack of love and procreation; and we develop and hold religious beliefs because we fear death. We really don't consider these actions as being fear driven, but in a subtle way they are.

And there is the fear of imminent danger. When we are faced with life threatening situations, we feel the sudden strong and terrifying emotion of fear. Probably this fear serves no purpose in many instances; however, in many other cases it may stimulate life saving action.

Ben R. Leonard, M.D.

Fear creates one of life's greatest paradoxes – it is the driving force of cowardice and the driving force of bravery.

What a fantastic thing is fear! We are damned and blessed with it, but on balance more blessed.

Forgive

Dictionary Definition

"Cessation of resentment against an offender; Pardon; To give up resentment of or claim to requital for an insult."

Beyond the Dictionary

What a marvelous thing it is to forgive and then, to put frosting on the cake, to forget.

When one has suffered a seriously egregious offense, it is very difficult to forgive, but there are modifying factors. If the offender is truly contrite and apologetic, then forgiveness is almost mandatory. If, on the other hand, the offender is unapologetic, forgiveness becomes a considerable task or impossibility, but still, for peace of mind and kindness sake, it is desirable.

There is no black or white to offending or forgiving. There are a multitude of ways and degrees to offend. There are fewer ways to forgive, and often forgiveness is more difficult, but nobility and a surprisingly calming affect lie in the forgiving.

It is a very disturbing thing to carry a grudge – even a justified grudge. When a person cannot find forgiveness, he or she becomes uneasy and often unhappy or saddened. To be unable to forgive the contrite shows a mark of instability, of insecurity, and possibility of unkindness. One should always try to forgive and grasp at every possibility to forgive and even try to create the possibility.

When forgiveness has been accomplished, it is time to forget the offense. This is often, if not always, the most difficult task because memory lies in a deeper part of the mind than the conscious act of forgiving requires. Forgiveness is the necessary conscious act; forgetting is the unconscious luxury that our mind may or may not allow. Fortunate is the person whose mind allows this luxury, but still more fortunate is the person whose moral judgment demands forgiveness.

Ben R. Leonard, M.D.

I quote an old and wise adage by Alexander Pope: "To err is human, to forgive, divine."

Friend

Dictionary Definition

"One attached to another by affection, esteem, or love."

Beyond the Dictionary

The word friend conjures up in my mind some wonderful thoughts and memories. I shall explain later.

A friend is really more than an attachment by affection or esteem; although, there are those elements in friendship. A true friend is someone you can trust, someone you can depend upon in tough situations, someone who will go out of the way to help, indeed someone who shares affection and esteem and a special kind of love.

Short of family, a true friend is one of your most important possessions. Yes, I said possessions because in a very unique way friends own one another. You don't buy friendship; you earn it in hundreds of different ways. Friendship is a society of mutual giving and receiving without keeping score. Friends need only the return of love they give.

I consider myself to be a very lucky man to have had and to have the wonderful friends who have graced my life. A good number of them have passed on, and I miss them terribly, but they live on vividly and indelibly in my memory – such fantastic and beautiful memories. Bless them for blessing me.

And there are still some lovely friends who are alive and sending their great vibes my way both personally or from afar.

How wonderful it is to know that there are those on this old earth who would do anything possible to make my life safe and comfortable! And they know the feelings are mutual.

Even though I'm not much of a praying man, I try daily to send some wish, call it a prayer, for the safety and happiness of those I

Ben R. Leonard, M.D.

am honored to call friend here on earth and for the comfort of the souls of those who have gone.

Do you hear me up there, Guys?

Gluttony

Dictionary Definition

"Excess in eating or drinking."

Beyond the Dictionary

"Thou shouldst eat to live; not live to eat," said Marcus Cisero, but Cato the Elder said, "It is a difficult matter to argue with the belly since it has no ears." Ah, Gluttony! Deaf and dangerous!

Food is basic to life, and at the beginning of man's existence was used solely for this purpose. As humans evolved, our capacity for pleasure also evolved and increased. After thousands of years of eating and drinking for sustenance, we began to find variety and pleasure in eating – eating became delightful dining. Soon eating became festive and a part of our celebrations – a way of life!

With food becoming more varied and tastier it was bound to follow that some would get caught up in the joy of eating and would carry it to extremes. Thus was born gluttony. Too bad!

Gluttony is looked upon as sinful by some, but I disagree. There is no harm done to others by the glutton save perhaps his or her family and less harm to them than to the glutton.

Unquestionably, gluttony is a health hazard. Resultant obesity, hyperglycemia, hyperlipidemia, etc. can and do cause serious health consequences, physically as well as emotionally and mentally.

Gluttony is habitual almost to the point of addiction – it becomes a compulsion. It is extremely difficult to cure, and requires first the realization and acceptance by the affected that he or she is a glutton, then the honest and determined desire to be free of the affliction. This is only the beginning. The treatment phase requires extreme self-control and determination for a prolonged period of time. Treatment of gluttony is akin to the treatment of addiction and requires a similar amount of time and effort on the part of the treated and the physician and staff. Often it takes a full team to treat and cure gluttony.

Oh, man! If only food didn't taste so good!

God

Dictionary Definition

"Supreme or ultimate reality; The Being perfect in power, wisdom, and goodness whom men worship as creator and ruler of the universe; The incorporeal divine Principle ruling over all as eternal Spirit; A being or object believed to have more than natural attributes and powers and to require man's worship."

Beyond the Dictionary

I cling to the definition of God as the creative force of all things both finite and infinite and thus omnipotent. God created us and, as the omnipotent force, can wield power and determination over our total disposition.

God, with this infinite power, has imbued humankind with the ability to feel, think, reason, and act. God has given each of us a spirit and a soul. From this point things become a bit mind-boggling to me, particularly when considering the dictionary definition of God which states that He [She/It] is perfect in wisdom and goodness.

Is it wise or good to allow or create poverty, famine, devastating storms, war, or criminal acts? If God is omnipotent as he must be, is he good simply by the virtue of power? Many, if not all, religions claim that God is good and loving; therefore, not only deserving of but also demanding of being worshiped. I have trouble with this. I'm not sure that God expects worship. If such were the case, God would eliminate evil and devastation.

There are those that argue that God gave us the power of reason and independent action and that all egregious acts and conditions are man-made. They argue that we bring on our own punishment. Does this apply to the starving, insect ridden, tortured infants and children? God! Omnipotent? Yes! Good and loving? I wonder. Could God not have made this a kinder, gentler, more peaceful world?

Ben R. Leonard, M.D.

I respect God and the great creative power and thank Him [She/It] for life and my personal good fortune on earth, but as much as I would like to, I have difficulty worshiping. I could be wrong.

Greed

Dictionary Definition

"Excessive or reprehensible acquisitiveness; Excessive, insatiable desire for wealth or gain."

Beyond the Dictionary

It's tough not to be a little greedy. We all have wants and desires often in excess of the norm. Some of us want a bit more money than we need; others want a home fancier than the average, or a better automobile, or nicer clothes. Well, what the heck! So it's a bit greedy. So OK. But it's not OK to be grossly or covetously greedy.

There is always the chance of big trouble when inordinate desire rears its head. If the greed is overwhelming, chance goes out the window, and trouble becomes fact. Often there are terrible rifts in interpersonal relationships, sometimes leading to physical and/or financial harm.

If the greed is on a larger scale, there is often damage done to big corporations and their investors, to societal organizations, to communities, to nations, and even to the world.

Corporate officers can often be so greedy as to create ecological damage in order to increase their profits or to actually embezzle at the expense of many trusting employees and investors.

Embezzlement by leaders of organizations or by the lowest of volunteers or employees almost invariably causes harmful results.

Greed by politicians constitutes a serious violation of trust and often creates damaging consequences. Perhaps I judge too harshly, but I tend to indite, in my own mind, most politicians as being greedy. Thank goodness our country is big enough and strong enough to withstand their greed for power and money.

Ben R. Leonard, M.D.

The most egregious and damaging greed is that of some national leaders. They often lead to plunder, terror, and war.

Happily for the USA, most of these leaders have been from foreign lands, but we've had a few. Without greed the world would be a much happier and secure place.

Hate

Dictionary Definition

"Intense hostility and/or aversion usually deriving from fear, anger, or sense of injury."

Beyond the Dictionary

Hate is a terribly intense and demanding emotion – so demanding that it's not worth the mental, emotional, and even physical effort. Hate leaves the hater drained, and rarely does it do the hated any damage other than that of hurt feelings and an enemy. When hate wanes, it often leaves no chance for reasonable debate and resolution. In short, it is probably the most destructive of all emotions.

If my conception of hate is true, then why do humans hate? I feel that hate is a learned phenomenon, taught to us by both those we emulate and those who offend us.

We observe our parents and other role models express their emotions, and we adopt like mannerisms and emotions. If we have exceptionally exemplary mentors, we learn to handle those who abuse us with calmness, thoughtfulness, and dignity.

If, on the other hand, our mentors are less thoughtful and more prone to anger, we tend to develop similar characteristics. However, I do not believe these observations hold the whole answer.

There can be acts against us so egregious that hate is almost a mandatory response. Even if our role models have been flawless, there are events that demand hate. I cite a few examples: the killing or torture of loved ones, rape, and ravaging and plundering societies or groups of people. Thus, the killers, rapists, terrorists, and unbridled dictatorial tyrants all teach us to hate. This is a hate that is well earned, but even this hate should be tempered with a certain control, deliberation, and thought.

Ben R. Leonard, M.D.

If we have a justifiable hatred without thought and consideration, we run the risk of unjust or destructive response or unproductive response. Try not to hate, but if you must; then, above all else, THINK!

Health

Dictionary Definition

"The condition of being sound in body, mind, and spirit – esp. free from physical disease or pain; The general condition of the body."

Beyond the Dictionary

Your health! Guard it with your life! Sounds funny, doesn't it?

But it's no laughing matter. Many bask in the sunshine of good health only to be stripped of it for no good reason.

Certainly, at this point in time, we can do little to alter our genetic structure – perhaps in the future, but not now. We can be cautious, but accidents happen and contagion exists. There are disease entities beyond our control. We recognize and acknowledge these things, and can only hope for the best.

Yet there are conditions of poor health that we create or enhance. Are we stupid or just too careless or hedonistic to act preventively? I've been in the practice of medicine for over 50 years and have yet to really know the answer, but I can cite some facts and offer some advice.

Tobacco smoking is a killer! That's the straight of it! Smoking is extremely damaging to the vascular system with devastating effects to all other systems, particularly to the heart and lungs. If I could only tell you of the terrible heart disease, the emphysema, the lung cancer I have witnessed, you would be appalled. Nicotine is addicting, but addiction can be broken; life cannot be resurrected.

Booze! Good old alcohol! Sure, it actually has some benefit to health if taken in moderation, but watch out! The stuff can sneak up on you and destroy your life physically, mentally, and emotionally. Moderation is not only the key, but the necessity.

Ben R. Leonard, M.D.

Street drugs or uncontrolled prescription drugs can be addicting and ruinous to health, both physical and mental. For the life of me, I can't understand misusing drugs. My Gawd! Why?

Exercise, proper diet, and moderation. Don't smoke! No illicit drugs!

Heaven / Hell

Dictionary Definition

Heaven : "Dwelling place of the Deity and the joyful abode of the blessed dead; A spiritual state of everlasting communion with God."

Hell : "Nether realm of the devil and the demons in which the damned suffer everlasting punishment."

Beyond the Dictionary

Oh, Wow! How I wish I could be a true believer! On the other hand, if the concepts of Heaven and Hell be true, how do we know to which we will be assigned? We are told that if we are good, Heaven awaits; if we are bad, Hell awaits. And there are those who place the added restriction that we must believe in the Holy Trinity to make it into Heaven.

The Big Question is who developed the Heaven / Hell theory. My understanding is that it comes from mortal sources, from those who could not possibly have been to either place. Were they divinely inspired? How do we know? It is possible, but the question remains, how do we know?

My thoughts: We, each of us, have a soul and a spirit. Both serve us temporally with the spirit tending our thoughtful needs and the soul tending the deeper, more transcendent needs. It is inconceivable to me that death simply turns off the soul. I feel that the soul goes on in some way that I, as a mortal, cannot imagine. If my conception is true, what happens to the soul? Heaven? Hell? Nirvana? Valhalla? Etc.? Etc.? Or does the soul simply float through some transcendental ether?

You will notice that I pose more questions than answers. This is because I am nothing more or less than a human being. There are so very many religions and philosophies that I find it impossible to pick one as the "True One." I want to believe in something; so I have developed my own philosophy as noted above. And I do strongly feel that being a kind, concerned, charitable person will give one an edge in the hereafter whatever that may be.

What a presumptuous SOB!!!

Hedonism

Dictionary Definition

"Doctrine that pleasure or happiness is the sole or chief good in life."

Beyond the Dictionary

Oh! Oh! This hits pretty close to home in the author's younger days. Fortunately I did not totally subscribe to the doctrine of hedonism, but I must admit that I spent beyond my means and failed to adequately prepare for "The Golden Years."

There are those of us who tend to want pleasures beyond the accepted norm. We seek happiness without appropriate thought to the future. I don't think this makes us bad people – just a bit stupid in the ways of future survival.

There are varying degrees of hedonism. There are those who completely destroy themselves in seeking "The Good Life" with utterly no conception of what the consequences may be. There are others who work hard and feel they are due a degree, perhaps inordinate degree, of pleasure and happiness. They tend to be too lavish in life-style, yet they are a bit more temperate. I consider myself to be of the latter group. The difference is probably only a matter of degree.

As I sit here in my 76 year old body, I tend to view hedonism in a different light. I never considered myself to be hedonistic as a young man. The trouble was that I, as so many youths, felt immortal, indestructible. The future seemed so very distant – I could plan for tomorrow tomorrow!

Well, my viewpoint has changed possibly in great part due to the way I view happiness. Yesterday happiness was excitement, going places and doing things, sports and parties.

Ben R. Leonard, M.D.

Today happiness is loving my family and friends, seeking knowledge, imparting knowledge, working, healing, and helping. What a difference the clock makes.

Now I observe hedonism and say," How very shallow and foolish, but scold me, do not scorn me."

Holy

Dictionary Definition

"Set apart to serve God or a god; Characterized by perfection and transcendence; Commanding absolute adoration and reverence; Filled with superhuman and potentially fatal power."

Beyond the Dictionary

To be holy seems to be rather awesome. As we commonly perceive holiness, it can only exist in superhuman modality. It would seem almost impossible for holiness to exist in human form – please note I use the word almost because I feel that holiness as we usually think of it is possible for a human to achieve but not probable, and indeed, highly unlikely.

Having said the above, I can only ascribe "Holy" to our creator, God if you will. I have no difficulty with the descriptions of "Characterized by perfection and transcendence" and "Filled with superhuman and potentially fatal power." What bothers me is the description, "Commanding absolute adoration and reverence."

As I have stated elsewhere in these essays, I believe in a creative force, and God is a perfectly appropriate name for that force. I am in no position to judge whether God is or is not perfect – I do see what I perceive as many imperfections in God's creations, but how does one judge? Unquestionably, God is transcendental. Being the creator of all things God is superhuman, and it follows God must have fatal power.

Here's the rub. Given that God is all powerful, why has He/She/It allowed so much suffering and tragedy in the world? Does the creator of all this misery warrant absolute adoration and reverence? Does our Creator really want or expect this from us?

Holy? Yes. Commanding of adoration and reverence? I say no, fully aware there are those among the readers who would say I blaspheme. Yet, if I do inadvertently commit blasphemy, I do so

77

Ben R. Leonard, M.D.

with a benign and questioning mind fully aware that there is a Holy entity.

Homosexuality

Dictionary Definition

"Manifestation of sexual desire toward a member of one's own sex."

Beyond the Dictionary

Far too much is made of sexual desire and the differences between heterosexuals and homosexuals. It seems to me that all of us should have the right to love and be loved by whomever we choose. That men mutually love, that women mutually love, or that men and women love one another or, for that matter, that there are bisexuals is no one's business other than the people directly involved.

I must admit that I disapprove of too much open display of sexual affection. I believe there are some things better kept private. I also believe that crass public display of sexuality is, to some degree, offensive. I do not want someone else's mores shoved down my throat or the throat of any human – there should be some sense of decency.

I also believe in basic human equality. I realize there are many who believe that marriage should only occur between men and women. Even most dictionaries describe marriage as a union between members of the opposite sex; however, I strongly feel that homosexuals should have the right to a legal union with all the rights and privileges of marriage. I'm not so adamant that homosexual unions be called marriage, but on the other hand, to call such unions marriage does not offend me. It seems merely a matter of semantics, and to vehemently insist one way or the other strikes me as being juvenile or paranoid.

There are two valid sides to those who disagree about homosexuality. Those who find homosexuality a bad thing find their point validated by the homosexuals who are crass and demanding. Those who do not find homosexuality bad tend to

Ben R. Leonard, M.D.

be more moderate in their judgments and more in accord with a justice for all attitude. I see both points of view, but tend to agree with the latter.

Live and let live!

Honesty

Dictionary Definition

"Fairness and straightforwardness of conduct; Uprightness of character and action."

Beyond the Dictionary

There are few, if any, character traits more valuable or desirable than honesty. The person who wishes to live in harmony and peace with all other humans must be honest.

There are laws against certain types of dishonesty as there should be. It is dishonest to steal and to harm another physically, and these offenses can be lawfully punished. They are not honest actions. We all know this, and most of us try to avoid these offenses.

There are other types of dishonesty such as lying, cheating, infidelity, disloyalty, and immorality. Some would dispute the inclusion of all or several of these as being dishonest to which I would have no quarrel. They might wish to call all or several simply immoral and exclude immorality from the definition of dishonest. This might be splitting hairs, and for the sake of this particular argument, let me call them dishonest.

In a sense, hurting another person or other persons in any way is being dishonest, and to carry the argument a step farther, any intentional act to harm one's self is dishonest. So being entirely honest is a big and difficult order.

It would be nigh impossible to find an honest person if held to the strictest definition, and yet there are many honorable people who have broken the rules. Humanity or being human demands that we be allowed some slip-ups and be forgiven some of our more human transgressions and still be perceived as honest. "Let him who is without sin cast the first stone."

Honesty in the strictest sense is seldom, if ever, achieved; however, those of honorable intention may be seen and thought of as honest. The point is that we should all strive to be honest.

It pays! And, as an added bonus, it makes you feel good!

Honor

Dictionary Definition

"A good name or public esteem; Showing of merited respect."

Beyond the Dictionary

To live an honorable life is to be kind, to be generous and giving, to be productive, to be serving, to be honest, and to be loving. No small task! But there are people who have those rather special and spiritual qualities, and they earn and deserve public esteem - Honor.

First and foremost, one must have integrity to gain the full respect of fellow humans and to be honored by them. Honesty is one of life's most important and desirable qualities. If a person lies, cheats, steals, or intentionally harms another human being; there is no chance for honor.

Kindness and generosity and the willingness to serve are also requisite to honor. Those willing to give of their possessions and selves for the sake of humanity gain not only the respect of others but also a deep sense of personal satisfaction that kind and generous acts always provide. People who are greedy and niggardly with their time and money are never admired or respected. For them there is no chance for honor.

Our life's work is so very important to gain not only a living but also respect. We must be productive, serving human beings to gain admiration and the proper regard of our families and communities. Slothfulness brings no reward, and for the indolent there is no chance for honor.

To be truly honored, love is equal in importance to integrity. The person who loves his or her family, friends, community members, and humans everywhere is the person most likely to be loved in return and to be honored. These people exude a certain spiritual aura of goodwill and devotion to humanity. We honor them.

Ben R. Leonard, M.D.

Paradoxically, those we most honor generally are those who least expect it.

Hope

Dictionary Definition

"Cherishment of a desire with expectation of fulfillment."

Beyond the Dictionary

Hope, it seems to me, is a bit more uncertain than to be a thing of fulfillment expectation. Hope is more desire than expectation, yet expectation is a part of it.

The beauty of hope is its positive attitude. It is almost invariably directed toward something good or desirous. We hope for love, for good health, for good friends, for a comfortable home, for nice clothes, for money, and for good things and events in our lives. It's a good thing to hope when hope is good.

There is a flip side to hope. There are those of evil intent who often hope for the injurious. In these cases it's good that hope is only hope and not fact. I may be a "cock-eyed optimist," but I think there are more good hopes and dreams than bad.

As good as hope can be, it really is not quite enough. Fate undoubtedly plays a role in the fruition of our hopes and dreams, but it's best to take some insurance. The insurance is work.

Anything worth hoping and wishing for is worth working for. The person who only daydreams lives in a tenuous, uncertain world – a world likely to be disappointing and unfulfilled. The person who hopes and dreams and works towards those goals is more likely to see success and fulfillment and, thus, happiness and contentment.

Of course, there is a caveat. There are things we can only hope for with little or no way to exert any influence by work or other means. We may wish for good health only to be stricken with disease or accident. We may wish for rain only to have drought, or we may wish for sun only to have rain. We may wish for peace only to have war.

Ben R. Leonard, M.D.

In spite of the bad, there is more good. Keep dreaming, hoping, and working, and may it all be for the best!

Hypocrisy

Dictionary Definition

"Feigning to be what one is not or believing what one does not."

Beyond the Dictionary

Hypocrisy is never honest, but it can be benign. Whether it is benign or malignant depends on two factors: the reason and the results.

All too frequently there are those who are hypocritical for nefarious reasons, for their personal gain or the gain of some project or cause. I know that I tend to pick on politicians, but I think they deserve derision as a class. Many politicians pretend to espouse or agree with causes or projects with which they disagree simply to curry favor with their constituents or with someone who might be helpful to them. This is malignant hypocrisy.

Then there are those who pretend for their own aggrandizement or self gain with no thought to harm anyone else, and in fact, they do no harm or minimal harm to others. These are typified by the office or work place "brown nosers" and the "teachers' pets." They really mean no harm, and may do no harm. At the worst they may displace a fellow employee or distract attention from another student. Maybe we should label these the "In-betweener Hypocrites" – neither truly malignant nor truly benign.

Next we get to the actors. These are the people who are unsure of themselves and brag with a bit of exaggeration. Almost everyone sees through them, but there's no harm done. They're benign.

Then there are the kind hypocrites who tell "little white lies" to make others happy or to avoid offending. They are the ones who call ugly babies pretty, tell homely people how beautiful or handsome they are, and tell the handicapped how smart or clever they are. These are the hypocrites that make the world a better

Ben R. Leonard, M.D.

place. Hopefully there is a little of this kind of hypocrisy in all of us.

Imagination

Dictionary Definition

"The act or power of forming a mental image of something not present to the senses or never before wholly perceived in reality; Creative ability; Creation of the mind."

Beyond the Dictionary

What a wonderful and powerful thing imagination is – a creation of the mind in combining one's knowledge, experience, needs, and desires. Imagination is a toy, a demon, and a magnificent tool.

Who among us hasn't been a Walter Mitty? In our daydreams we can travel to foreign lands; we can walk the surface of the moon or visit the stars; we can fly with the birds or swim with the fish; we can be a fantastic athlete, a movie star, or the bravest of heroes. What a beautiful toy is this thing imagination.

But woe to the person who imagines impending danger! The imagination can play some pretty terrible tricks on us if our mind becomes sickened or our thoughts distorted. Just consider how terrifying it would be to, for no reason, think you were about to die or suffer some calamitous event.

Without imagination there would be no war or the weapons of war. Yes, imagination can be a demon!

However, think of what this world and our modern society would be without people with great imaginations. There would be no castles, palaces, skyscrapers, magnificent bridges, and tunnels. There would be no automobiles, trains, airplanes, rockets, and ships. There would be no television, radio, telephones, and computers. There would be no electricity and the multiple devices that require electricity. There would be no stores to sell us the things we need or think we need or simply want. There would be no medicines, hospitals, doctors, nurses, and paramedical personnel. There would be no homes with the myriad devices for our comfort. For the lack of professional farming, which takes imagination, there would be no food other than what we could grow, hunt, and gather ourselves.

Wow! Imagination! More toy and tool than demon!

Immigrant

Dictionary Definition

"Person who comes to a country to take up permanent residence."

Beyond the Dictionary

As I consider Immigration and Immigrants, I find myself very ambivalent. Living in California, I see a state being over-run by immigrants many of whom receive far more benefits than they earn.

Our state, as many other states, has a huge financial deficit. An important difference between California and many other states is our border location and our large involvement in agriculture which allows for a tremendous influx of immigrants. We are now a state of 36,000,000 people. We are providing state financed medical care, education, and other welfare benefits to a multitude of people.

On the other side of the coin, it is a fact that we need a cheap labor force. Immigrants supply this – they work for low wages and do necessary menial work that few regular citizens would even consider.

Illegal immigrants are a separate and important consideration. I have rather strong feelings about the law, and I feel we should exert every effort to block illegal entry into our country and to apprehend those who we were unable to block. They should not be given welfare, education, and other privileges. They should be sent home.

What is the answer? Difficult!

We should tighten our borders even if it means using the military. We should exercise every effort to apprehend the illegals and stop winking at employers who pay them under the table.

Ben R. Leonard, M.D.

We should thoroughly examine our labor needs, establish a quota system, and demand that immigrants follow the rules of entry.

Oh, well, what the hell! It ain't gonna happen!

Intelligence

Dictionary Definition

"Ability to learn or understand or to deal with new or demanding situations; Ability to apply knowledge to manipulate one's environment or to think abstractly as measured by objective criteria."

Beyond the Dictionary

Very frequently the words Intelligence and Knowledge are confused as meaning the same thing, which is, of course, wrong. Intelligence is innate; knowledge is acquired.

How lucky are those who have been assigned the genes allowing for superior intellect. I feel that intelligence is gene linked. We tend to see highly intelligent people in the same family just as we see families with generally lower IQ's. Certainly there are exceptions to these observations. From time to time, families of lower intellect will produce a genius, and conversely, highly intelligent families will produce an idiot.

There should be no pride to superior intellect nor shame to diminished intellect. The genetic structure we inherit should not be subject to judgment; however, what we do with the intellect given us is important and will be judged. It is up to each individual to use his/her intellect as best it will allow – to develop skills, to effectively think and rationalize, and to gain as much knowledge as possible.

Perhaps the assignment of degrees of intellect is of divine design. Maybe the "Big Boy" decided that we humans need those to handle the planning and management of earthly matters, those to develop scientific progress, those to philosophize, those to entertain, those to handle the manual work, and those to handle the menial work. Why not? The Creator, God, seems to have had a "Grand Design." Why not include the assignment of intellect as a part of that design?

OK! You have intellect. Now use it!

Jealous

Dictionary Definition

"Intolerant of rivalry or unfaithfulness; Disposed to suspect rivalry or unfaithfulness; Apprehensive of the loss of another's exclusive devotion or loyalty; Hostile toward a rival or one believed to enjoy an advantage; vigilant in guarding a possession."

Beyond the Dictionary

What an unhappy state is jealousy! It can be, and often is, emotionally devastating, particularly in the lives of marriage partners and lovers.

Jealousy is caused by any of several factors. It can be the result of infidelity or presumed infidelity. It is often the bitter fruit of an unstable or insecure personality. Some people are basically distrustful, and tend to build imaginary scenarios the truth of which only they are certain. Others hear of or actually observe actions by their mate which indicate infidelity. Their jealousy is more firmly based and more credible; however, either condition of jealousy is psychologically damaging.

Once someone becomes jealous, it is imperative that it be addressed in a calm and sensible manner if the relationship is to remain loving, effective, and with a reasonable degree of trust. If this approach is impossible for any reason, the relationship is doomed. This is not always easy, but it is imperative.

Needless-to-say, jealousy is never good under any circumstances, and mental and emotional control always lead to a more desirable outcome for everyone. Guard your emotions with deliberation and temperance – regardless of the circumstances, you'll be happier.

I have not addressed the jealousy often felt toward a gifted rival or in guarding one's prized possessions, but suffice it to say, it stems from a basic insecurity, can be emotionally devastating, and in virtually every instance, leads to nothing good or desirable. Neither do I address the psychodynamics of etiology in detail, but

Ben R. Leonard, M.D.

I do advise the attempt at reason and emotional control. Why make yourself unhappy?

Kill

Dictionary Definition

"To deprive of life."

Beyond the Dictionary

God, what a simple definition for such an important act – an act of finality – termination.

The longer I stay on earth, the more abhorrent I consider killing. Perhaps aging with its proximity to death gives one a greater appreciation of life. Living is quite a gift. Some lives are sweeter, more peaceful, more successful, more complete, or more satisfying than others, but with some exceptions, life is good and to be desired. Killing is taking away this great gift. Killing is wrong.

Generally, we think of killing in the context of taking a human life. Possibly this is as it should be, but again as I age, the thought of killing other animals troubles me. I am particularly distressed by hunters killing those creatures of the wild just for the sport of it. Killing is a sport? What is this instinct in man that makes him want to kill? I have trouble understanding.

Yes, I know, I eat meat, but killing animals even for food is beginning to trouble me. I still condone it in my own mind with the rationalization that we need some meat protein in our diet, but really, do we? I know, I know! I'll probably continue to eat meat, but my rationalizing doesn't completely clear my conscience. Still killing animals for food is far more rational than killing them for sport.

Back to people. It seems to me that the more advanced society, local and world, has become with its guns, bombs, and magnificent weapons of war the less feeling we have about killing. We humans have killed such a multitude of people that we're becoming inured to killing. My God!

Ben R. Leonard, M.D.

I have but a few words about the "Death Penalty." Killing is wrong no matter who does it. There are better ways to punish which are worse than death. Life in a cell is far worse than being killed. Good God! Why must we keep on killing?

Kindness

Dictionary Definition

Kind: "Of a sympathetic nature; Inclined to be helpful and solicitous."

Beyond the Dictionary

Kindness is another of those traits to be learned, but I suspect there is more to it than just learning. I suspect there must be something inherent in the human spirit that allows us to absorb the quality of kindness. True, we must be taught, but we must be receptive. Once kindness becomes a part of us, there are few, if any, qualities that are finer or more desirable.

Imagine what this world would be like in the absence of kindness. There would be no charity – the hungry would starve, the homeless would have no refuge, the sick would suffer and wantonly die, and the helpless would perish. I know that, in spite of the kind efforts of many, there are those that will starve, remain homeless, suffer and die, yet the kind keep trying.

What a shame that kindness has not been infused into every person on earth. Just think of the monumental good that could be done if each one of us extended a hand of help to those in need. Unhappily, not all are kind which keeps the world that much farther from being perfect.

Kindness is a marvelous gift to have. There is no feeling on earth to equal that of being helpful and giving to those in need and to see the gratitude in their eyes. The feeling of love and warmth that the kind of heart display comes back to them many fold. Their ability to selflessly help their fellow humans and to care and protect the animal world is priceless both to the recipients of their kindness and to their own spirit and soul.

To understand the importance of kindness, consider what the world would be like if all individuals were of the nature of Hitler,

Ben R. Leonard, M.D.

Stalin, Caligula, Hussein, Amin, and Chong-il. What a tormented existence we all would have!

Whatever else you might be, strive to be kind.

Knowledge

Dictionary Definition

"Fact or condition of knowing something with familiarity gained through experience or association; Acquaintance with or understanding of a science, art, or technique; The fact or condition of being aware of something; The range of one's information or understanding; Sum of what is known."

Beyond the Dictionary

OK, you're intelligent. So what? Being intelligent is only the beginning because there is so very much to know, and knowing comes only through exposure to experience, to education, to study. Intelligence is not knowledge - knowledge must be acquired, and the harder and more diligently one works at it, the more knowledgeable one becomes.

There is no shame to being retarded in intellect and without knowledge, but there is great shame in being very intelligent and without knowledge. The latter implies a slothful character, poor motivation, and a basic disinterest in life and the world and all of their wonders. What a terrible waste to one's self and to society to have a superior intellect without the knowledge to be productive and beneficial, to be of service to self and others.

Admittedly, knowledge is not always easy to come by. Often it takes years of higher learning to gain the know-how to do the job for which one is destined. Often it takes demanding and even terrible experiences to gain the knowledge requisite to perform one's calling in life. Most frequently it takes both experience and formal education.

All the above being said, it really is not important to be highly intelligent. It is more important that one use his or her God-given intelligence to gain the amount of knowledge that his or her particular intelligence will allow and then to use that knowledge to live a good and productive life.

101

Ben R. Leonard, M.D.

My advice: Don't be lazy. You've got a brain. Use it! Get yourself some knowledge!

Law

Dictionary Definition

"Binding custom or practice of a community; Rule of conduct or action prescribed or formally recognized as binding or enforced by a controlling authority; The whole body of such customs, practices, or rules."

Beyond the Dictionary

Law – It is the force by which we can reasonably live together as humans with different beliefs, customs, needs, and desires. Without law society would be allowed to run rampant – the strong could rule the weak, and the smart could rule the unintelligent. The law with its rules and regulations tends to create a more equal living condition for society.

No one is so naive as to believe that our laws give us complete immunity from danger or harm. There are, and will always be, those who feel they are above the law and are dishonest or immoral enough to break the law. Some will actually avoid apprehension and punishment, but others will suffer the penalties of law. There are enough of the latter to give pause to those who might contemplate violation of the law. Thus, law, with its rules and punitive measures, serves both as a deterrent and a mode for punishment. Importantly, it also provides a means to determine the type and degree of criminal punishment, unfortunately not always wisely or fairly.

Just consider what our lives would be like without our laws and law enforcement measures. We might all be carrying guns for self-protection, and even worse, we might be experiencing the unfettered effects of that weapon of mass destruction, the automobile. Of course, I say the latter partly sarcastically, but there is an element of truth. Without law there would be nothing to contain the unlawful or the unruly element of society.

Admittedly, there are flaws in our justice system, particularly in the area of penalty. In one region of the country punishment for the same crime may vary vastly from another region. In fact, there are even differences in what is considered a crime. "Let the punishment fit the crime" is subject to many interpretations.

Law is not without flaw, but liberty demands law.

Liberty

Dictionary Definition

"Quality or state of being free; Freedom from arbitrary or despotic control; Positive enjoyment of various social, political, or economic rights and privileges; Freedom."

Beyond the Dictionary

How marvelous it is to be free - - - to have Liberty! There is no greater right than that of liberty. How very lucky we are to live in the United States of America!

Just consider those parts of the world ruled by monarchs or dictators. Their people are subjugated to the whims, desires, and rules of one or few without the power to decide how they will be governed or who will govern them. If their ruler is evil and despotic, they may be tortured, imprisoned, or even killed for little or no offence. They are completely at the mercy of the one who governs. Can you imagine such a situation here in the USA?

Our forefathers fought for and won liberty for us. We were born into freedom; it's in our blood. If anyone seriously tries to take our liberty, there will be a fight. I abhor war, the killing and the dying, but liberty is the most important cause for fighting a war.

Recently there has been enacted the "Patriot Act" here in America. I am not entirely familiar with its contents, but it has been suggested that it significantly increases the surveillance and investigative powers of our law enforcement agencies without adequate provision for the checks and balances to safeguard our civil liberties. This indicates to me that if this Act is used and abused by less than honorable authorities, our liberty is in jeopardy.

My years of action and protest are about ended; indeed, my years on earth are numbered; so my peers in age and I leave the future to the young. It is my hope they will be alert, diligent, and active in preserving their liberty. Without freedom life is hardly worth living.

"Give me liberty, or give me death!" Ol' Pat was on target!

Life

Dictionary Definition

"Quality that distinguishes a vital and functional being from a dead body; Organismic state characterized by capacity for metabolism, growth, reaction to stimuli, and reproduction; Period from birth to death."

Beyond the Dictionary

Wow! What a word is life with all of its implications. What a marvelous miracle is that of birth, of living and of dying for all things, plant and animal. So how can we refute the existence of a creator – God, if you will? But this is not about the creator; it's about the created.

I won't address vegetable life even though it is a fascinating subject in itself. I do find animal life, particularly human, more compelling and interesting.

My life has been devoted to the physical aspects of the human body which remain fascinating and still something of a mystery to me, but far more wondrous and mysterious is the psyche. What a fantastic thing it is to think and to emote.

The living body is indeed a thing of beauty in its design and function. Consider, if you will, the multiple systems we have which must all work in harmony – the brain and nervous system, the heart and vascular system, the kidneys, the lungs, the gastrointestinal system, the musculoskeletal system, the endocrine system, the sensory organs, the genitalia and reproductive organs, and integument. What a wondrous machine of flesh and bones we are!

Then give this machine of flesh and bones the ability to think, to feel, to emote – just consider the magnitude of this creation! How astounding! Who or what could have the intellect and power to create human life? It's beyond imagination, and yet here we are living, breathing, thinking, emoting – just a mundane everyday affair is life – that is, unless you think about it!

Wow! What a thing is life!!!

Love

Dictionary Definition

"Strong affection for another arising out of kinship or personal ties; Affection and tenderness felt by lovers; Affection based on admiration, benevolence, or common interests; Warm attachment, enthusiasm, and devotion; Unselfish, loyal and benevolent concern for the good of another or others"

Beyond the Dictionary

True as it is, the dictionary definition of Love seems too stilted. Love almost defies definition; it is such a strong emotion. It is the emotion most of us strive for -to love and to be loved.

Not only is love a many splendored thing; it is also a many faceted thing.

There is physical love which is perhaps the most superficial of the facets, yet so greatly desired that it becomes a near necessity and engenders deeper emotional ties which often become the basis of good, strong families. Closely akin to physical love is the affection and tenderness felt by lovers and often mutated into the love of the lovers' family. Love is the bonding element of the family - without it there is no strength to hold the family unit together - without it there is a loss of concern which is devastating to the moral fiber of each family member and the family as a whole.

Love is the concern for dear friends born of mutual interests, mutual desire to serve and please one another, and trust in one another. Without friends to love, and to thereby have a mutual dependency, life would be a much less desirable state. Family is wonderful, but to multiply that wonder, one must have friends to love.

Then to reach the emotional depth of the truly mature, thinking, benevolent person, one must love mankind and all of nature.

That love must manifest itself in action –to express one's love for all that exists is well and good, but to act on that love is near divine. It is so very important to reach out with one's time, skill, and finances to help those in need or to help and preserve those of God's creation who might be suffering. Love, the root of all good.

You may note that I have not alluded to the love of or for God. This is because I have difficulty in my particular belief in God which I discuss in other chapters. Suffice it to say that I have a strong belief in God, the creator, and a great respect for God, but I'm not sure that love, in my philosophy, applies. In this area I live in a world of troubling doubt. Does my honest questioning disqualify me for Heaven, if Heaven exists?

But I do love and have little malice in my heart. Perhaps this will allow my soul a peaceful journey someday.

Love and live to be loved. That's the ultimate happiness – the ultimate life!

Marriage

Dictionary Definition

"Institution whereby men and women are joined in a special kind of social and legal dependence for the purpose of founding and maintaining a family; An intimate or close union."

Beyond the Dictionary

These are pretty dry words in the dictionary to describe what should be one of the closest, if not the closest, human relationship.

Marriage should never be entered into lightly or without serious deliberation. Then, what's the problem? The problem is that too many of us are often too young; too many us "Fall in Love" without thinking; too many of us expect marriage to equal constant, unending happiness.

Youth! If luck prevails, we get through it with our single hides intact, or we fortuitously marry the one who just happened to be Mr. or Mrs. Right. That leaves the rest of us who are either the smart deliberators or the not so smart thoughtless romantics – The first class may make marriage work; the second class may also but only with heaps of luck and rather sudden maturation.

Many will find themselves in the divorce court wondering what hit them.

OK! Here's the advice of one who's been there! Keep your eyes and your mind wide open. Never presume. Always evaluate and question. If there is the slightest doubt, back off! Life is full of other opportunities.

Once you are sure as you feel you can be, say, "I do," and mean it. Next comes the real lesson! Life is not a bowl of cherries; so how can we expect marriage to be? It ain't! Believe me!

Bowl of cherries or not, marriage can be wonderful, but it takes some work. Why not? Anything in life truly worth having is worth working for. The most important rule: "Expect less than you give, and you'll get more than you expect." Simple as that.

The primary characteristic required of marriage partners is Love. If love exists, then will follow concern, respect, understanding, forgiveness, and the physical closeness so very important in a successful marriage. The first four above are a given. The last is sometimes the first to be lost, and what a pity it is to lose that wonderful and happy closeness that comes from touching and feeling - the marvelous feeling of lying side by side in bed.

But all else failing, remember: "Expect less than you give."

Maturity

Dictionary Definition

"Quality or state of being mature – especially fully developed."
Mature: "Having completed natural growth and development."

Beyond the Dictionary

Maturity implies far more than a fully-grown body. In fact, this is only the surface of maturity. Real and full maturation requires the mental and emotional processes to be fully developed. This is a big and important order and not always achieved.

It is not important that we have a very intelligent mind to reach maturity, and we need not be extremely thoughtful; although, thinking helps. It is of paramount importance that we have a concerned mind in order to reach full maturity.

Maturation is a process of change – change from the "Me Attitude" to the "We Attitude" to the "Thee Attitude." That's it! Maturity is the attitude of concern. It's the developed ability to want food, clothing, shelter, education, security, and safety for all of humankind. Until you have this concern, you are not mature.

This wonderful maturity develops slowly in some and, unhappily, never in others. There are those who remain in the "Me Attitude" all of their lives. They never reach maturity, they tend to be a drag on those who try to love them, and they never reach a complete state of contentment and happiness. There are those who get stuck in the "We Attitude." They are able to function a little more effectively, to raise a family, and to have a relatively reasonable cocoon existence.

The truly mature individual is he or she who cares for family, friends, and all of society and societies – the "Thee Attitude" individual. These are the people who know the fullness of life and the ultimate maturity and happiness.

Ben R. Leonard, M.D.

My wish is that we could all reach this wonderful state of concern for all things, great and small!

Medicine

Dictionary Definition

"Science and art dealing with the maintenance of health and the prevention, alleviation, or cure of disease."

Beyond the Dictionary

I recognize there are multiple definitions of "Medicine;" however, I have taken the liberty of using only the one that describes the practice of preventing, alleviating, and curing. The obvious reason for this is that it is my profession, and I am pleased and proud to have practiced for over 50 years.

It requires dedication and a certain philosophy to practice medicine. First, and most importantly, any physician who wants to practice effectively must put his/her patients in the position of prime importance. This means the patient is more important than the physician's time and pocketbook.

Though dedication to patients is number one, there are other qualities necessary to the practice of medicine, and in fact, they all relate to the importance of the patient:

> Honesty - An imperative - Every patient deserves and should expect to be treated with honest regard for his or her diagnoses and treatment and for the cost of that treatment. Further, if mistakes are made in either diagnosis or treatment, it is the physician's honest duty to admit to and to the best of his or her ability correct the error. This last is very difficult in the litigious age we live in, but it is imperative.
>
> Fairness - A good doctor treats all people equally without regard to class or status and with every measure available.
>
> Concern & Compassion - Every patient deserves as much freedom from harm and pain as is humanly possible, and the physician must feel the need and desire to supply this freedom.

115

Continuing Education - The amount of knowledge to be had in medicine is staggering and increasing daily. Reading medical books and journals, listening to audio-programs, viewing computer programs, and attending medical meetings are absolutely necessary. One wonders if the human mind is capable of grasping and holding all the information that has been and is being developed to practice medicine. Whether we can or not, it is an absolute necessity that we try, and I feel that most of us do a pretty reasonable job of learning the required material to handle our particular medical specialty.

Physical & Mental Stamina — The long and demanding hours required to practice medicine are part of the "Doctors' Lore." Any person who decides to become a doctor must fully understand this and must develop the mental and physical toughness to withstand a lifetime of stress.

I have addressed those qualities required of physicians, but it is important to recognize nurses and all other paramedical personnel who play such a very vital role in health care. I feel it important to say that they require the same qualities as noted for physicians.

In my long years of practice I have seen and dealt with a multitude of medical and paramedical people, and with few exceptions they met the above noted criteria.

I'm very proud to be a part of this wonderful team of people and very happy and satisfied to have been given the opportunity to serve my fellow humans.

Medicine is a great and emotionally rewarding field. I'd do it again!

Money

Dictionary Definition

"Something generally accepted as a medium of exchange, a measure of value, or a means of paying."

Beyond the Dictionary

It's true that money isn't everything, but in our system of exchange it is very important. We no longer barter as in days of yore. We work for money. We pay our bills with money. Without money we eat, sleep, dress, and live in poverty.

One of life's most difficult tasks is living relatively comfortably while saving enough money for the times of disability or senile debility. Many have found this to be almost impossible due to several reasons. My experience leads me to the conclusion that immature reasoning coupled with a touch of hedonism account for most failures to save enough money. There is the youthful "I'm going to live forever" Syndrome which leads to the "Live for today; Tomorrow is but a dream" Syndrome which, in turn, leads to the misuse of money. Ah, how easy it is to fall under the spell of this youthful philosophy and later find that the roof over your head, the food in your mouth, and the clothes on your back are all more than you can afford. You didn't put some money away!

Certainly, life must have some pleasures, but they must be reasonable pleasures. We must be cautious. Eat some of the fruit from the tree now, but put some in jars for the days to come. Save some money!

Yes, money is important and fun to have, but perhaps the greatest lesson to be learned is that our greatest pleasures come from simply being with family and friends, from cuddling your pet, from searching the stars, from resting and running by the sea, from admiring the grandeur and beauty of the forests and mountains. These are the things that money can't buy.

And never forget the wonderful feeling of helping those in need.

We must all try to keep enough of our money to satisfy our needs, but most of us have some to spare. Giving a part of your money to the poor, the hungry, the homeless is incredibly rewarding, both to the one who receives and the one who gives.

I haven't mentioned "The root of all evil" side of money. There is no question that a great deal of dastardly things has been done for the gain of money: embezzlement, bribery, lying, cheating, and theft to name a few. Let's just hope that more good than evil is being done for and with money.

Regardless of who or what you are, you need a certain amount of money. My wish for all is that you have enough for your needs, for your happiness, and for your charitable spirit.

Music

Dictionary Definition

"Science or art of ordering tones or sounds in succession, in combination, and in temporal relationships to produce a composition having unity and continuity; Vocal, instrumental, or mechanical sounds having rhythm, melody, or harmony."

Beyond the Dictionary

Ah, what a wonderful world of sound and beauty the word "Music" conjures. Just run through your mind the marvelous melodies, rhythms, and lyrics that have been a part of your life. To exist without music is unthinkable.

We use music to celebrate our birth and birthdays, all the happy events in our lives, our religious ceremonies, our local and national holidays, our weddings, and just to celebrate the joy of living.

We use music to express our emotions, to vent our feelings, and to communicate in a very special and magical way with rhymes and rhythms. We use music to express our sad and unhappy moments. In some mystical way music helps to lift unhappy spirits from our shoulders, to calm our fevered brows, to soothe our sadness, and lighten our losses.

Not least, we use music to entertain. Life is wonderful, but it is no bed of roses. Who among us doesn't need some respite from our daily humdrum? Music can and does offer us this source of restful entertainment. How wonderful it is to clap, swing, sing, and dance to a lively tune. How lovely it is to sway to the sounds of a romantic ballad. How marvelous it is to bathe and bask in the sounds of a beautiful symphony or ballet or the sounds of a single instrument or voice or chorus of voices.

We need music! Without music I think our spirits would wither and die. Thank God, melodies, rhythms, and lyrics will continue to flood our lives with their wondrous sweet liqueur.

Ben R. Leonard, M.D.

I really haven't said enough about music because not enough can be said! Music! It's magic!

Obscene

Dictionary Definition

"Disgusting to senses; Abhorrent to morality or virtue."

Beyond the Dictionary

There is a time and a place for everything. I guess this includes obscenity. There is such a variety in mores, beliefs, and sensibilities that the meaning of obscenity is multifold. What is obscene to one person may be simply humorous or a natural part of living to another.

Pornography is seen as obscene by many; by others it is nothing more than a depiction of natural instincts, albeit an exaggerated depiction. To curse or use the name of God in vain is considered obscene by many; just as many use "obscene" language in a flippant manner with no thought of it being obscene. There are those of us who consider sport killing to be obscene; there are probably many more who simply feel it natural to kill wild animals. There are conservative members of several religions who feel homosexuality is obscene; there are others of us, who tend to be more moderate, who feel that homosexuality, though not mainstream, is not obscene.

I cite the above examples to illustrate the many differences of opinion regarding what is and what is not obscene, but there are some noteworthy agreements.

I think we all agree that rape is a terrible obscenity, that torture is an obscenity, that child pornography and any abuse of children is an obscenity, and certainly that wanton killing is an obscenity. Probably the degree of egregiousness determines the difference between varied versus universal impressions and beliefs about obscenity.

Regardless of what a person feels is or is not obscene, there is the question of consideration and respect for one's fellow humans. We should always be cautious and considerate of the sensibilities of each other. Be as comfortable as you wish in your view and use of that which might be considered obscene by another, but be considerate. Why offend when there is no need?

Pain

Dictionary Definition

"Basic bodily sensation induced by a noxious stimulus, received by naked nerve endings, characterized by physical discomfort [as pricking, throbbing, or aching], and typically leading to evasive action; Acute mental or emotional distress or suffering."

Beyond the Dictionary

Pain! We must all deal with it. It's part of the price we pay for the privilege of living. Although, there are those who pay more dearly than others and some for whom the price is too high.

Physical pain is, in fact, more easily dealt with than mental or emotional pain. Physical pain simply, admittedly at times quite harshly, reflects something agley with our body. It is a warning that something should be done, frequently the first warning. As a herald that we should seek diagnosis and treatment, pain is our friend. Fortunately, in this modern age, pain can more frequently than not be diagnosed, and treatment modalities are generally available and adequate.

Mental or emotional pain is more demanding to tolerate. Diagnosis is often quite obvious as with the response to personal loss of a loved one or important material possessions, or diagnosis can be extremely difficult as with endogenous depression or anxiety or psychosomatic disease. Treatment modalities are psychotherapy, drugs, and often "tincture of time." Prognosticating is often more obscure than for physical pain. We can usually predict when a broken limb, a laceration, a sore throat, a kidney stone, or even a bad back will stop hurting or when the pain will diminish or not. Not so in mental or emotional illness.

Pain tolerance is a large factor in both psychic and somatic pain. To use an old cliché, "Everyone is different." It is amazing to see the terrible pain that some individuals can endure and the minimal pain that others seem unable to tolerate.

123

Ben R. Leonard, M.D.

What a wonderful world it would be if we all caused no pain and assisted when we encountered pain.

Parents

Dictionary Definition

Parent: "He or she who begets or brings forth offspring."

Beyond the Dictionary

Parent is so simply defined for one of life's most important individuals with one of life's most complex jobs. What greater and more significant task is there than raising children?

What are the qualities requisite to being a good and effective parent? Above all the ability to love followed by concern, compassion, selflessness, honesty and integrity, diligence, steadfastness, discipline, equanimity, fairness, understanding, and unbounded energy – and I've probably missed a few, but I think I've conveyed the idea.

Parents are far and away the most important element in the upbringing of children. They out rank teachers, friends, and all others. This is not to denigrate the role of others, rather to stress the importance of parents.

From the moment an infant is cradled in the arms of a parent, it begins to feel and learn love, security, and belonging. These same sensations and emotions are conveyed when we tuck our children in their beds, feed them, clothe them, touch them, and teach them. The most important emotions and rules in life are taught by parents.

Parents teach both directly and indirectly. Children learn by being directly shown or told how to do the myriad tasks involved in communicating, eating, dressing, playing, singing, dancing, and dealing with people and situations. They also learn indirectly by imitation; they learn by observing the conduct and habits and by listening to the talk of their parents.

Parents are the first and most often the most important role models for their children. If they are good and honest, clean and healthy, educated and well read, their offspring are likely to emulate. The same may be said for those who are dishonest, immoral, unhealthy and unclean, and poorly educated.

Gawd, how wonderful to be a parent! Or how terrible!

Passions

Dictionary Definition

"Emotions as distinguished from reason; Intense, driving or overmastering feelings."

Beyond the Dictionary

Passion! Good and bad! Love is a passion; hate is a passion!

In spite of the bad, there is great good in being passionate because passion is the source of our ambitions and the driving power to bring them to fruition. Just imagine what our world would be without the great theories and inventions, without our magnificent bridges and highway systems, our transportation systems, our communication systems, our space exploration, and our marvelous medical advances to name only a few of the world's great achievements. All of these and so much more have been accomplished by intense, driving passion.

And humankinds' most precious gift is the ability to love and be loved – what a wonderful passion. It is the driving force of procreation, of families, and of peace. It is the driving force behind most of the world's religions and behind our desire to care for the needs of others, both animal and human.

There is passion in joy, in kindness, in charity, and in all goodness.

Oh, yes! Hate, anger, jealousy, envy, etc. are passions. These are the destructive ones! These are the passions which destroy both the passionate and the recipient of the passion. It seems to me that the world would be so much better if these passions did not exist, but then perhaps not.

Perhaps it is a part of human nature to need contrast – maybe we require difference. Maybe we need to be angry as well as to be loving, perhaps there is a requisite greed to give credence to to our charity, and maybe there is a human need for war to make us appreciate peace.

We humans are a peculiar lot! We probably couldn't handle utopia.

Patriotism

Dictionary Definition

"Love for or devotion to one's country or nation."

Beyond the Dictionary

Being a patriotic American makes it a little difficult to view patriotism as those of other nations might feel; however, I imagine that the emotion is just as strong in all countries where government has been kind and just.

One does wonder how patriotism is felt or perceived in countries run by dictators or suppressive governmental entities. There must be a sense of devotion to the land of one's birth, but it would seem that some of this devotion could be dampened or even obliterated by a tyrannical government.

How should and to what extent should patriotism be expressed? In 1816 Stephen Decatur said, "Our country! In her intercourse with foreign nations, may she always be in the right; but our country, right or wrong." I agree that we should be steadfastly devoted to our country, but I strongly feel that when our leaders have acted unjustly or wrongly in our name, we have not only the right but also the duty to protest and demand correction. There are those who feel such response is unpatriotic. They rigidly subscribe to the "Our country, right or wrong" concept. I must just as strongly disagree with this concept. No matter who commits a wrong, it should be corrected.

Does this make me unpatriotic? Absolutely not! I would fight to the death to protect this land that I love and its freedoms. This includes the freedom to protest that which I feel to be wrong.

In recent days there has been some abuse, or at least misuse, of governing power in the United States. Protestors have been labeled unpatriotic and even treasonous. I admit that some of the protestation seems to go too far, but those who would stop it also go too far. This is the nation built on freedom which includes freedom to protest and to speak. It seems to me those whose protest is honest can be patriotic, and those who would deny the freedom to protest and speak are probably unpatriotic.

"America! Love her or leave her!" Yes, but never deny our rights!

Peace

Dictionary Definition

"State of tranquility or quiet, Freedom from civil disturbance; Freedom from disquieting or oppressive thoughts and emotions, State or period of mutual concord between governments."

Beyond the Dictionary

Peace. There is such a beautiful tranquility in the word. Peace. It is so very much to be desired. Yet we in this beat up old world have seldom, if ever, known a time when there was total peace.

What is it with mankind? We all desire peace, but we incessantly fight. Is it greed, hunger, jealousy, or just plain stupidity that makes us want to harm, mutilate, terrorize, plunder, and kill one another?

Talk to your next door neighbor, to the people down the street, to almost anyone you meet in the course of an average day, and ask them if they prefer peace or war. The universal answer is peace unless you're talking to a nut. Virtually no one wants war, but we allow our leaders to attend their hostile agendas and blithely march into battle.

I recognize there are times when we must fight to gain peace, safety, or security, but I also recognize that in many instances war could have been avoided with deliberation, reasonable discussion, and intelligent statesmanship. Let us hope and pray that wiser heads will prevail in future national disagreements,

Wars do harm. They destroy lives, property, economies, and minds. Wars make good people killers and plunderers. I will continue to ask why war and why not peace until the day I die.

A peaceful world is bound to be a more fruitful, more productive, healthier, wealthier, and happier world.

Ben R. Leonard, M.D.

Why can't we kick our national and world leaders in their stupid asses and make them realize this?

MY GOD! WHERE ARE THEIR BRAINS? And their hearts?

Pet

Dictionary Definition

"Domesticated animal kept for pleasure rather than utility."

Beyond the Dictionary

Pets are a subject near and dear to my heart. There is little in life more comforting than sharing your life with a pet. Please note that I said sharing your life as opposed to owning a pet.

I say it in such manner as to emphasize how important it is to be kind and caring for our pet or pets. I'm not some nut who does not recognize that we own our pets, but I am some nut who feels that pets must be handled with kindness and love.

Pets can teach us how to expand our love beyond human love. They offer us an extra outlet for our ability to care and have concern for another living creature, to broaden our ability to love.

I must confess that dogs are my favorite pets with cats running a rather distant second. These are my choices based on my own individual experience. I'm sure people who own and care for other furry creatures or birds or reptiles are just as sold on their pets with a loving and caring attitude being the driving force.

And so to dogs! This is my experience – not trying to sell anyone on dogs or away from their pet of choice. I love my dog! Next to my wife and children, she is the most important living being in my life. She is a member of my family. We are constant companions. I sense in her a love for me that transcends the logical. We seem to communicate without a word – she knows my moods; she knows when I hurt; she knows when I'm happy; and she responds. In turn I try to keep her happy and out of harms way, and I think she knows how much I love her.

I am simply trying to communicate to the reader how important it is to fully expand your capacity to love, and pets offer us this wonderful opportunity.

Always, always be kind to animals. They live on this earth with us. Let's share it with love and kindness.

Politician

Dictionary Definition

"A person experienced in the art and science of government; A person engaged in party politics as a profession."

Beyond the Dictionary

Well, here goes nothing! And I hold my nose as I write! As you undoubtedly have already gathered, I'm no great admirer of politicians. But I should explain.

I have watched politicians of all ranks, sizes, and shapes in my 76 years, and with few exceptions, I distrust them. I feel that it takes two basic traits to become a politician: greed and the need for power. Rare is the individual who enters the political arena for altruistic purposes, and those of that bent often falter along the way.

I believe the chief and driving force to become a politician is the need to control – the need for power. Politicians, as a general rule, feel that they know what is best for society and are willing to go to unusual lengths to achieve that "best." They bend the truth or frankly lie to serve their agenda or to stay in office.

If greed is not the initial motivating force to enter politics, it soon becomes one of the dominating factors in maintaining political office. As a result, wealthy special interests have a far greater influence on those who govern us, and thus how we are governed, than the general public.

Adding to my condemnation of greed are the multiple perks that many of our representatives receive in the way of free health benefits, the franking privilege, no overhead in the conduct of their business, and spectacular retirement benefits.

If all politicians were brought into our Social Security and medical programs as average citizens, you can bet there would be a dramatic change in the way the average citizen is treated.

Ben R. Leonard, M.D.

Admittedly, there are some good and honest politicians, but they are few and far between. My general impression of politicians can be summarized with one word: Ugh!

Politics

Dictionary Definition

"The art and science of government; The art and science concerned with guiding or influencing governmental policy; The art and science concerned with winning and holding governmental control."

Beyond the Dictionary

Politics, it seems to me, is less science and more art. All too frequently government is controlled by appealing to the emotions of the people rather than to their intellect. This requires more artistic skill than scientific knowledge. Of course there are exceptions. There occur infrequent times when the public demands explanation – such times as entry into wars which seem unwarranted, unusually heavy governmental expenditures, unusually high taxation, questionable intrusion of government into private lives, etc. Questions such as these should be answered in a clear, precise, scientific manner. We, the voting public, should expect no less.

Unhappily, our political representatives do not always give us straight, honest facts. All too frequently we are served up lies as facts. This is in great part our own fault. We have indolently allowed ourselves to believe in politicians and in the hog-wash they spew forth as truth.

At this point you must be understanding my sentiments regarding politics which leads me to our "Two Party" political system in the United States. Some things good, some things bad! The good part of a specific political party is its ability to furnish us a political platform and people to run for political office. The bad part is the very same thing – political parties tend to tie us to a specific policy and furnish us people to control our government over which and whom we have had little or no say. I feel the bad outweighs the good!

Ben R. Leonard, M.D.

My main objection to Democrats, Republicans, Greens, Libertarians, etc. is that each one has a rather firm philosophy and agenda – carved in stone! This often leads more to thoughtless argument than to constructive thought and discussion. I personally cannot abide this. I am an Independent!

Pornography

Dictionary Definition

"Depiction of erotic behavior intended to cause sexual excitement."

Beyond the Dictionary

I have no quarrel with pornography if it is used wisely and judiciously by adults in privacy. I feel that people of age, for the sake of argument let's say beginning somewhere between 18 and 21, have the right to see pretty much anything they want.

It is too bad that some adults become dependent upon porn for sexual arousal. It can become an obsession. In such event the affected can almost, and in some cases definitely, be considered mentally ill with an obsessive-compulsive disorder - the equivalent of a mental addiction. These are people in need of medical / psychiatric intervention unless they have enough moral and intellectual strength to control their habit.

The greatest and most deserved condemnation of pornography concerns its use of children. This is an abomination. I must admit that I have never seen child pornography, but viewing such immoral filth is not necessary to condemn it.

Also, I feel it immoral to allow children to see pornographic material. Children are not emotionally mature enough for explicit sex. They need to be allowed their childhood with its gradual maturation process. They need thoughtful parental guidance.

All of the above being said, I still feel that pornography should be an adult prerogative. There is no particular harm in being aroused sexually, and porn can provide one of the avenues to that arousal. I have no compunction in viewing porn myself, and have done so on rare occasion - the caveat being that I have no driving need to do so.

My advice: Use pornography only as an adult, never with a minor, and not so frequently as to become jaded or obsessed. In the final analysis, porn has little or no real value but does little or no harm if used judiciously.

Poverty

Dictionary Definition

"State of one who lacks the usual or socially acceptable amount of money or material possessions; The state of being very poor or destitute."

Beyond the Dictionary

I have considerable difficulty with defining the state of poverty. I understand there is a certain level of income considered to be below the acceptable level or to be in the poverty level. I'm not certain that this is a true measure of poverty, and yet I have trouble defining true poverty myself. I have always thought of poverty as being more abject than it seems to be considered here in the United States. Probably this is a good thing for Americans. It implies that our standard of living is much higher than that of many other countries; therefore, our poverty level is higher. This is not to imply that we do not have those in an abject level of poverty. We do, but there is aid available here, and there is always a glimmer of hope in this land of plenty.

True terrible, abject poverty, it seems to me, is that which exists in many of the Latin American and other Third World countries. As we all know, there are areas of the world where men, women, and children have only the hint of living quarters, tattered or no clothing, and insufficient food to maintain health or life. What makes this horrible situation even more devastating is the fact that there appears to be no relief.

What a terrible shame it is that there is so much waste in this world. We spend billions of dollars on useless food, superfluous clothing, fancy houses and automobiles, and most wasteful and shameful of all, WAR!

What is it with us, as human beings and a nation, that we can spend so recklessly and uselessly while people starve to death?

141

Ben R. Leonard, M.D.

Is there a final retribution? Are we damning ourselves with our flagrant misuse of our abundant goods and materials?

At the very least, we should hang our heads in shame. My heart breaks at the thought of someone dying for the lack of the food that I throw away. I hope that some day, some how we can correct our error.

Power

Dictionary Definition

"Possession of control, authority, and influence over others; Physical might; Mental or moral efficacy; Political control and influence."

Beyond the Dictionary

Power! What a tool! It can be used for good or for evil. This goes without saying, but the interesting and important thing or things about power are the types of power and the modes of obtaining and keeping it. Parental power, political power, religious or spiritual power, legal power, mental or emotional power, physical power, financial power – and I expect I've missed some. All of these types of power can bring about wonderful things or terrible things.

Political power is confounding to me. I have become very jaded and dubious in my regard for politicians. I have grown to feel that they seek office to gain power. This being for personal gain or satisfaction, more often than not, results in misuse of power.

Spiritual power allows religious or cult leaders to lead transcendentally, to direct morals, and to give hope. This is a wonderful and uplifting power in the right hands and can go far in creating better people, better communities, better nations, and a better world. In evil hands it is one of the most destructive powers known to man.

Mental or emotional power is that exerted over a weaker person or society akin to the power of dictators and cult leaders. Seldom is it benign. Often physical power is used concomitantly. The results of this power can be devastating.

Financial power has seen some of the most benevolent and some of the most heinous manifestations. Wonderful humanitarian charities and foundations have seen the beneficial power of money. On the other hand, our governmental leaders have often been led into nefarious projects and actions detrimental to their constituencies and to their country by the power of money.

Observation: Those who seek power tend to abuse it.

Pray

Dictionary Definition

"To request of a deity in a humble manner; To address God or a god with adoration, confession, supplication, or thanksgiving."

Beyond the Dictionary

Prayer is a difficult thing for me to discuss. It requires more than a modicum of introspection. I must consider my impressions and feelings toward religion and God. As I have stated in the essay on religion, my views and feelings are secular, but I do believe in God as our creator but not a specific god. I have difficulty with the concept of worship with the notion that God may not expect worship. As before, I hasten to note that I could be wrong and that I simply do not know. Yet, in my own way, I pray. I know there is a tremendously powerful creative force, God, if you will, and I sense that force is omnipotent, therefore, cognitive and capable of response; so I silently and at times vocally talk and supplicate to our creator. I don't know! Sometimes I think I'm a bit nutty! But I think as I think and believe as I believe and seem to have no intellectual or conscious control over these processes. Does anyone?

Now my thoughts regarding prayer in general: Most people who pray do so as a believer in a specific god, and that is a good thing. First, it can do tremendous good for the psyche. It can and does bring peace to depressed, anxious, and troubled spirits. Prayer has a wonderful soothing and calming effect. Second, prayer often has a psychological effect, allowing or causing the praying individual to act in such a way as to effectuate that for which they supplicate. In a sense this is the power of suggestion – self-suggestion. Some might suggest this concept to be a sacrilegious view of the power of prayer; however, it may be God's way of answering supplication.

I feel that most who pray do so with a spirit of good will or at least with benign intent; therefore, prayer is likely to do some good. If those who are evil pray, let us hope our Creator has the grace to turn a deaf ear and protect the product of his power.

If your prayers are thoughtful, respectful, and benign, why not?

Procrastinate

Dictionary Definition

"To put off habitually and with intention; To put off intentionally and reprehensibly the doing of something that should be done."

Beyond the Dictionary

Gawd, it's easy to procrastinate! Show me the person who says he or she has never procrastinated, and I'll show you a liar or someone with a memory about one millimeter long.

Just recall all the onerous or boring tasks you have been called upon to do over the years, and remember how easy it was to say tomorrow, often for more than one tomorrow. We have all procrastinated at some time or another.

For the simple, unimportant tasks putting off until manana is usually OK, but procrastination on the "Big Things" is an absolute no-no! Procrastination on things of importance can cost jobs, loss of huge amounts of money, and even loss of human life.

Human nature is a very peculiar thing. Most of us want to get our jobs and projects done, but there seems to be a lazy, let's do it later streak in us. This is particularly true for the unpleasant tasks, but it even applies to those that give us some pleasure. This is just another one of life's little mysteries – at least to me.

Certainly, there are plenty of people who are serious and diligent and who recognize the important things and get them done, but I'll bet a nickel that even they procrastinate on the little things at times.

As I say, I'm uncertain as to the psychodynamics of procrastination. Maybe it's just plain old laziness which is an ingrained trait, to a greater or lesser degree, in most all of us.

Ben R. Leonard, M.D.

Whether we know the cause or not, we do know that procrastination is one of the things that keeps the world of man from moving too fast — [and the world of woman to be PC.]

When procrastination does no harm, maybe it's a good thing at times.

Psyche / Soma

Dictionary Definition

"Soul, Self, Mind." / "The body of an organism."

Beyond the Dictionary

What a fantastic combination! The psyche and the soma! Put the two together, and voila, the human being! What a marvelous admixture of flesh, blood, and bones with mind and soul! There has to be extant, albeit unseen and transcendent, a creator with intelligence and omnipotence to have created man and woman, to have given them the power to physically motivate, the brain to guide that motivation, and the power to think and feel and emote. OK, let's call him [or her or what?] God. The name is unimportant. The existence of a creator is of infinite importance, but I digress.

The Soma, the human body, is quite a remarkable creation – a mass of various materials to make organs and systems to effectuate those organs in such a way that we can move about, work, play, and perform all the functions required to live our lives. The human body is nothing short of a miracle.

But the miracle to top all miracles is the human brain – the leader and driver of our bodies. The brain is the seat of our Psyche – our mind, spirit, and soul. The mind allows us to feel, think, perceive, and will. The spirit gives us the quality of sentience which guides and controls our emotions. The soul is the most marvelous of all the gifts given to mankind – The essence of our existence. If my presumption is correct, the soul gives us immortality.

It's a shame [or is it?] that there are flaws in our psyches and somas. Mental and/or physical infirmities are a part of virtually every human life. Rare is the human being without illness. This is a fact that I have some difficulty understanding. I reason that God is omnipotent and of supernatural intellect to have created all of the wonders of the universe. So why did he create us so flawed? Is there some design in our defects and weaknesses? Are we imperfect by God's intent? Or did God just want to give doctors a way to make a living? I don't have the answer, do you? You may think you do, but I'll bet you don't!

Religion

Dictionary Definition

"Service and worship of God or a presumed deity or the supernatural; Commitment or devotion to religious faith or observance; A personal set or institutionalized system of religious attitudes, beliefs, and practices; A cause, principle, or system of beliefs held to with ardor and faith."

Beyond the Dictionary

I subscribe to all of the above definitions, and though my sentiments are somewhat secular, I do believe in a creative force and have no problem assigning the name "God" to that force. My problem with religion is the very diversity of religion. It is difficult, if not impossible, for me to accept Christianity with its many facets or Judaism or the multiple religions of the Near and Far-East and Africa as the one "True Faith."

Are we not all human beings, domestic animals, animals of the forest, or the multiple forms of flora? Do we not all live on the same planet? Can there be a separate God for each religion, each sect, each geographical area, each species? This just doesn't make sense to me.

In my view, admittedly a humble view of someone who has no higher authority, there can be but one creative force, God, if you will, to have designed and constructed this universe, this world, and all the flora, fauna, and minerals therein.

And yet, I have no quarrel with individual religions if they espouse love, kindness, charity, forgiveness, and hope through faith. My problem with specific religions is their dogmatic and closed-minded approach to life and other thinking and philosophies with the resultant havoc this has caused. Unhappily, many religions have been responsible for terror, torture, famine, and poverty dating to ancient times – and this unfortunately includes the Christian Religion.

Ben R. Leonard, M.D.

Any religion that adheres to the philosophy of "doing good" and "doing no harm" is a good thing for society in that it builds moral character and protects society. These religions should not be condemned; rather, they should be praised.

So I believe in what religion can do, but not in specific religions.

Call me a Pantheist [who believes in all kindly motivated religions] or an Agnostic, but not an Atheist. There is a God - I just don't have the supernatural power to exactly define or describe Him / Her / It. And I have trouble believing that other humans have or have ever had this power.

Retirement

Dictionary Definition

"Withdrawal from a position or occupation or from active working life."

Beyond the Dictionary

Retirement? Why? Many will answer: "I'm tired and want to rest" or "I'm bored and want more excitement" or "I simply want some change in my life." These are all valid reasons to retire; yet I feel sorry for these people. The implication in all these reasons is they don't like their jobs. They have labored long years employed in an undesirable situation – at best, undesirable – at worst, bad and unrewarding. Of course, there may be reasons of health to retire. This is also unfortunate, but in my estimation it is actually better than being locked in an undesirable job for many years of drudgery. And, of course, there are degrees of ill health some of which are devastating, but so is a boring, fruitless life of employment ultimately devastating.

Still, retirement remains the answer for most, and I can't quarrel with this "Golden Years" solution for them; however, wouldn't it be wonderful if we all enjoyed our work so much that retirement would become our last resort?

Now comes my argument against retirement. In many cases, if not the majority, retirees just fade away. They lose their incentive to live; they seem to give up. In my 50 years as a physician, I've seen countless numbers of delightful, intelligent people retire only to find their enjoyment of life diminish, their cognitive ability decrease, and in some cases their health become more speedily impaired.

Oh, I know, there are many cases of successful retirement, but my experience and my "gut feeling" tell me there are far more failed cases. Ok, I'll concede that at times even my profession can become hum-drum, but there are other venues to add spice to our lives even as we remain employed: sports, hobbies, writing, music, traveling, theater, community service, & family, family, family!!

Retire? Who me!

Revenge

Dictionary Definition

"An act of retaliation in order to get even."

Beyond the Dictionary

I guess all of us have wanted revenge at times. It's a natural impulse, and if not carried to extreme, can be justified in some cases. Having said this, I must say that revenge is rarely a good or reasonable thing.

If a person or persons harm or commit an egregious act against you or those dear to you, it is natural to want to get back at them, to get revenge. All too frequently the reaction is too quick. If revenge seems imperative, it is far wiser to wait, to think, and to reflect. Most importantly, the period of reflection is often a period of cooling off, a time when reason and wisdom prevail, a time when revenge might seem useless and perhaps even foolish.

If after a cooling off period revenge still seems imperative, it is important that "the punishment fit the crime" and that no serious or lasting harm be done. We must always remember that we cannot, or should not, take the law into our own hands. If an unlawful act has been perpetrated against us, legal recourse is the only logical and appropriate action – we are not judge and jury!

Terrible acts are frequently committed including murder, rape, torture, etc. When such atrocities are imposed upon us or our loved ones, there is an almost overwhelming desire for retribution. These are moments when it is imperative that we stop and think, realizing that adequate punishment can only be administered by our law enforcement system. There is a caveat in my estimation: If we are present or become immediately present to acts of terrible violence, it is a natural instinct to act, and often this action is equally violent and justifiably so. Perhaps this is better termed defense rather than revenge.

In summary, revenge is usually useless and foolish, but at times can be warranted. Even if revenge is justified, it should never be administered without reasonable thought or lawful action. We should use our heads, not our hearts.

Secular

Dictionary Definition

"Not overtly or specifically religious; Not ecclesiastical."

Beyond the Dictionary

The word "Secular" has more than just its meaning related to religion; however, I wish to address it only in this context. I do this because it has been used in recent times in a demeaning manner toward those who have an honest problem with formal religions.

In my mind, secularism is a rejection of formalized religion with the recognition that at least one religious denomination may [and I emphasize the word "may"] be based on fact, and perhaps there is some truth in all religions. I simply do not know.

In this connotation I feel that I am secular. I am not a critic of most religions, and I feel that many religions do a great deal of good. I simply cannot accept a single religion as the "True Faith." I discuss this in more detail in the section on religion.

My quarrel with many religious denominations is their insistence that they are absolutely right and that everyone else is wrong. This is a minor quarrel in my mind; however, it becomes a major quarrel when they insist on imposing their beliefs on others.

I also believe that the more fervent agnostics and atheists often tend to err in a similar manner by their insistence that any and all reference to religion be abolished from schools and public facilities, particularly in the United States.

It is my belief that the USA was conceived by people who were basically of the Christian Faith and quite a few reasonable secularists, and respect for them as well as respect for tradition almost demands that we allow the symbols of Christian Faith and the present faith of many, if not most, Americans to be displayed. I also hold the personal belief that other religions should be granted similar privileges simply because we are all Americans, and we should all respect one another. Why do we have to be so offensive and so easily offended???

Security

Dictionary Definition

"Freedom from danger, fear, and anxiety; Freedom from want and deprivation."

Beyond the Dictionary

Perhaps security is the most sought after of all values. There is comfort and peace in feeling secure - secure from physical harm, secure in love and human relations, secure in employment, secure in health, and secure in aging. Without security we find ourselves worried and troubled - without peace of mind.

The desire to survive is fundamental to human existence, and to survive we must work or have some means to supply our need for food, clothing, and shelter. We need the secure feeling that we will survive. Without this we lose hope and happiness.

Just as basic is our need for love and friendship. There is a very wonderful security in the knowledge that one has loved-ones and friends who can be counted on for emotional needs, companionship, and help. Just consider how lonely and unsure life would be without family and friends.

How troubling and unsettling it is to be in poor health. It is particularly worrisome and even frightening to have serious diseases - the feeling of insecurity is almost intolerable at times. What a great feeling it is to be pronounced cured or free of serious disease - a wonderful feeling of security.

As we grow older, our capacity for work diminishes, and more often than not, we are required to retire - some more willingly than others. Security is paramount in the thought and desires of the elderly. When the ability to "make a living" ceases, the need for a way to survive is of utmost importance - Security!

I would be remiss if I failed to address the security we need or want as a nation. We were frightened by 9/11, and we remain

159

frightened – so much so that we started a war and are willing to kill and be killed to protect our security. I am uncomfortable about preemptive war. I want security, but I would rather defend my freedom than be an offender. Am I wrong?

Senility

Dictionary Definition

"Quality or state of being senile; Physical and mental infirmity of old age." Senile: "Relating to, exhibiting, or characteristic of old age."

Beyond the Dictionary

The age of senility is becoming older with medical and life style changes and advances. 100 years ago one became senile at the age of 50 or there about; rare was the person who lived beyond that age. Today women live on average to the age of 80 and men to age 74; so I guess we can presume senility to begin in our seventies. That being said, it seems to me there is a better way to judge senility and that is on an individual basis.

Most of us look upon someone as senile if they are old in appearance, are weak and debilitated, and their cognition is slow or confused. Frankly, this does seem to me the better way to determine senility.

We all know people in their late fifties or early sixties who are already "old" – senile, if you will. And we know people in their late eighties and nineties who are mentally and physically active. How can these disparities be?

Genes! Genes! Genes! Those little critters in our germ plasm that control transmission of hereditary characters. They're the miniscule devils that can raise your cholesterol, make you fat, and a myriad of other bad things. By the same token, they can do the opposite – they can give you the traits to stay youthful and healthy. But genes are not the entire picture.

Life style! The way you live – the way you eat, what and how much you drink, the type and amount of exercise you get, whether or not you smoke, and even your living conditions and the atmosphere you breath – are all important to how you age, your general health, your cognitive ability, and how long you live.

Ben R. Leonard, M.D.

So if you want to reach senility in grand style, pick the right parents and live right!

Service

Dictionary Definition

"Contribution to the welfare of others;Being helpful."

Beyond the Dictionary

What would we do without those gracious people who serve others? Communities, towns, cities, states, nations and the world are service dependent. Lest I confuse, allow me to explain that I do not refer to service for a fee, rather service for free.

What a gracious, kind, and wonderful gift humanity gives to itself, the gift of service. Service to others requires, at the very least, some time and effort; and often it requires much more. And it requires a kind and giving heart. People truly dedicated to helping their fellow beings are the products of kind and giving role models. Service is a learned value, but it does take a receptive spirit and a desire to help. Perhaps these are learned values too; in fact, probably they are. So, you parents and grandparents and aunts and uncles and teachers, find a way to serve all those who live on earth; show your kids the way life should be lived.

Unhappily, there are multitudes of people and animals in need of help. Fortunately, there are many helpers in many forms and capacities. We have national and international organizations such as The Red Cross, The Salvation Army, The Rotary Club, The Lions Club, The SPCA, and The Humane Society. We have local and community church, school, business, and social organizations dedicated to service. And, quite beautifully, we have kind and generous individuals who of their own volition seek ways to serve the needy.

I recognize that some of our major national and international charity and service organizations have had some difficulty with personnel and with scandalous activity; however, these incidents are relatively rare. We must always remember that we are dealing with human beings; therefore, we must expect imperfection.

Ben R. Leonard, M.D.

In general, all who give of their time and energy so freely and selflessly are honest and honorable people.

All of these servants may carry themselves with pride and a deep inner satisfaction. This is their pay and all that they want.

Sex

Dictionary Definition

"Sexually motivated phenomena or behavior."

Beyond the Dictionary

In this essay I do not especially consider gender; rather I choose to address the acts of sex which include coitus, fellatio, cunnilingus, anal sex, etc. Of course, we recognize the gender differences in so very many aspects of life including the sexual acts, and this must be accorded due importance. For my purposes in this instance, I acknowledge that there are general differences between men and women in their thinking about and approach to sex. By the same token, there are multiple differences among individuals.

Sex is not, and should not be, a cut and dry phenomenon. Sexual acts should be stimulating, passionate, pleasurable, and loving, and whichever form or forms people opt to use, there should always, always, always be mutual consent. If there is not mutual consent, the act is no longer pleasurable and loving, and it becomes animalistic and at times barbaric. Only those with a sick mind enjoy rape - they should be prosecuted and treated.

I am aware that many believe any act other than coitus for conception is sinful. I disagree with this stance. I feel very strongly that what happens in privacy between consenting adults is only their business. For those who wish to have productive coitus only, fine. For those who wish to probe every orifice and use multiple variations, fine. It is imperative that we respect the rights of privacy and freedom of action so long as no one is hurt or loses freedom of consent.

Mind your own business! Be a lover, not a boor! Have fun!

Be fruitful, if that's you bag! But remember to save a little room on old mother earth for your grandchildren!

Soul

Dictionary Definition

"Immaterial essence, animating principle, or actuating cause of an individual life; The spiritual principle embodied in human beings, all rational and spiritual beings, or the universe; A person's total self; Moral and emotional nature; Quality that arouses emotion and sentiment; Spiritual or moral force."

Beyond the Dictionary

The dictionary definition just about says it all. But? But whence comes the soul? Who gave us this ethereal quality - this essence of our being? This brings us back to the question, "Is there God?" To deny there is a creator is to deny one's own existence; so if there is a creator, then why not give him/her/it a name: "God" seems like an acceptable choice. The name "God" is aeonian, used by believers and disbelievers alike. Obviously, the reader does not have to accept my thoughts as fact, but I believe in a creative force, and for the sake of argument, I'll call it "God."And I believe God gave each of us a soul just as defined in the dictionary.

Did our soul exist before we were born? Was it a quality floating in some spiritual essence waiting for us to be born, or did God just whip it up on the spur of the moment and assign it to our human being? It would seem strange to me if something so unique, something so spiritual [please allow me] could be finite. Please note, I'm not answering - just speculating.

What troubles me is the next question. What happens to our soul when we die? I repeat my speculative question: How can our unique soul be finite? Yes, our flesh and blood can be destroyed, can be killed, but our soul? Imagine, if you will, when the Grim Reaper takes your mortal remains, that your soul flies into the ether and continues to function through eternity. What a thought! Is there some form of existence after death? Those of the various religious denominations and sects claim to know. Perhaps they

Ben R. Leonard, M.D.

are divinely endowed, but I doubt it – they're human! Me? I don't know. I'm human too.

Ah, Sweet Mystery of Life!

Spirit

Dictionary Definition

"An animating or vital principle felt to give vitality to physical organisms; A supernatural being or essence; The immaterial intelligent or sentient part of a person; The activating or essential principle influencing a person."

Beyond the Dictionary

Many people confuse the spirit with the soul, and admittedly the two are closely akin, but there is a fine difference. I am presuming that I know the difference; however, I personally hold this presumption in question. I shall explain my perception, and you, the reader, may make your own judgment – as you should in most all matters.

The soul is the essence of our being, the source of our morals and deeper emotions. It helps us distinguish right from wrong, good from bad.

The spirit is, as noted in the dictionary definition, "The immaterial intelligent or sentient part of a person." It give us our "thoughtless thought" – our awareness. And it is the driving force of our soul's inclination to do the moral or the immoral thing – to live the good life or to live the bad life.

The soul is the plan to go, and the spirit gets us there. With a slightly different connotation, yet valid in my estimation, the soul is our conscience, and the spirit is a step toward consciousness. It is my opinion that the soul and the spirit are interdependent. To make a rather unusual judgment with a slightly different twist on the word, spiritual, I believe that the soul is more spiritual than the spirit, but they are both of vital importance to human kind.

Religions and philosophies serve as guides to our souls and spirits –sometimes for the good and sometimes for the bad. It can only be hoped that these guiding forces will lead us to a kinder, gentler, more thoughtful and generous world and that the evil religions and evil philosophies will finally be seen as so damaging to humanity that they must fail.

Sports

Dictionary Definition

"A source of diversion or recreation; Physical activity engaged in for pleasure such as athletic games."

Beyond the Dictionary

Sports are a wonderful part of human existence if used properly or a drag on society when used improperly.

Sports are at their best for humans when we are active participants. In being a sport participant we improve our physical condition, we often learn teamwork and "Good Sportsmanship," and we add another element of pleasure to our lives – all good things. I personally exclude any killing activity from my definition of sports!

And sports can be a delightful observer experience. When handled correctly, sports are marvelous entertainment. This is particularly true in the amateur field. There is little more enjoyable than watching family and friends compete in athletic activity or watching a school sporting event. This is only true when all players and all observers are considerate, polite, and recognize that sports are only games. Too much ego, too much hostility, and too much fervor can spoil a wonderful entertainment and physical outlet.

My harshest criticism of sports is in the professional arena. I have three basic complaints: raucous, discourteous, and often dangerous fan behavior in condoning and stimulating venues; poor and frequently abhorrent behavior by "Sport Stars;" and outrageous salaries paid to professional athletes. Nothing much need be said about the first reason above. Just watch a football, soccer, or baseball game and observe the fans in action!

Athletes often argue their lives are their own, but they are lucky, highly paid people. They are role models, like it or not.

When they act indecently or dishonestly, they send a negative message to our children. Enough said!!!

For their relative service to humanity professional athletes are grossly over paid. Again, Enough said!!! For moral reasons I rarely watch professional sports.

Strive

Dictionary Definition

"The devotion of serious effort or energy."

Beyond the Dictionary

Do you want to get somewhere in life? Do you want to finish a project or task? You'd better have ambition, but ambition isn't worth a cent unless you are willing to really exert some energy - - - to strive!

So many intelligent and talented people in the world fail to succeed. Why? How can this be? They are gifted. They have brains and the talent to do great things, but they don't. Some even have ambition, and still they don't succeed. Why? The answer is easy. They're lazy!

Lazy people get nowhere. They have no "get up and go." They refuse to strive. What a terrible waste this is to them personally, to their families, and to society. I feel sorry for these gifted but indolent people. They lose the respect of their family and friends and all who depend upon them, and they ultimately lose their self-respect.

What is the answer? I'm not sure I know. All I can suggest to them is THINK. Think of all the marvelous things they might accomplish if they would strive. Think of the good they might do if they would strive. Think of the respect they could earn if they would strive. Think of the wonderful legacy they could leave if they would strive. My God, just THINK! Will this work? On some, yes; on some, no, but the ones who think and decide to strive will make the miracle of life work.

And there is another aspect to striving. There are those who are not very intelligent or gifted, but they have ambition and the willingness to work. They strive, and they succeed; some succeed far beyond that expected of them. They are respected by others and, importantly, by themselves.

Ben R. Leonard, M.D.

Those who strive are the winners in life.

My advice: Get off your ass and work! STRIVE!

Success

Dictionary Definition

"Favorable termination of a venture; The attainment of wealth, love, favor or, eminence."

Beyond the Dictionary

Rare is the individual who doesn't wish for success in some way. And there are numerous ways to be successful.

We all want a certain amount of wealth. Most of us end up contented with enough for food, clothing, shelter, and a reasonable degree of security, but there are others who wish to be financially successful. They wish for more than enough to furnish them with the necessities, and if they have the brains, talent, and energy; often they achieve their goal. They are successful.

There are those who wish to be looked upon with favor and respect, and if they prove to their peers and society that they are worthy of respect, often their wish comes true. They are successful.

The people who aspire to fame and eminence must have a special trait or talent to bring their desire to fruition. This is a difficult area in which to claim success, and success is not often achieved. For them to claim this type of success, they must be gifted with the special talent to carry them to fame, or they must have the ambition, drive and energy to make it to the top in their field. Only these people are successful in this arena.

There are undoubtedly more ways to become successful, but there is one type of success that transcends all the rest. The individual who lives life to the fullest as a loving, kind, and giving person is successful. The individual whose family and friends love and respect him or her is successful. The individual who has been as productive and creative as his or her intelligence and talent will allow is successful. The individual who can approach death with composure and self-satisfaction is successful.

Ben R. Leonard, M.D.

We all have the road to success in the palms of our hands.

Suicide

Dictionary Definition

"The act of taking one's own life voluntarily and intentionally."

Beyond the Dictionary

This is a tough one for me. I have little or no moral objection to suicide whether it be with or without assistance, but I do have some reservations.

I can agree that the terminally ill person who feels helpless, hopeless, and burdensome may want to consider suicide. I can agree that the person with severe and intractable pain may want to consider suicide. These people may feel there is no other option, and probably this is true. However, and in my mind this is a big however, if these people have family and/or friends who deeply care for them and are willing to see that living until natural death is made meaningful and reasonably comfortable for them, I feel they are obliged to hang on to life.

The suicides that distress me most are those committed because of emotional or mental problems. In many instances these suicides could be prevented with concerned family and friend intervention and appropriate treatment. The problem generally is a lack of communication. The disturbed individual frequently hides his or her emotional pain, or the family/friends lack the perspicuity or understanding to pick up on the psychological signals. These suicides are more deeply tragic it seems to me.

As a long practicing physician, I have seen the opportunity to assist more than a few suffering individuals in their desire to "end it all," and I probably could have managed to aid in their quest with impunity. I could not do it, and the illegality of it had nothing to do with my refusal to assist. There is something deeply ingrained in my conscience that disallows my taking a life, and there is an additional factor: From the moment I took the Hippocratic Oath, I felt it my duty to help my fellow humans, and I cannot, in my own heart, break this vow. I simply cannot equate assisted suicide with the moral practice of medicine.

My heart cries for those tormented souls who must "end it all."

Taxation

Dictionary Definition

"The action of taxing." Tax: "A charge of money or other valuable property imposed by authority upon persons or property for public purposes."

Beyond the Dictionary

Who likes being taxed? No one! Who feels the need for taxation? Almost everyone! The rub is in the who, how, what for, and how much.

There is a vast difference in opinion as to who and how we should tax. The far left feels that taxation should be based on relative wealth, and the far right on simple percentage. Liberals want the wealthiest among us to pay a disproportionately higher share. Conservatives want the wealthiest to pay a proportionately higher share. Those of us who claim to be moderates see the wisdom in both arguments.

Certainly, one who proves intelligent and diligent enough to become wealthy deserves to keep a goodly amount, but this should be tempered with the need to assist those who are not fortunate enough to have the necessary traits to acquire wealth. There must be a middle road, or nations become two tiered with only the very wealthy and the very poor. This is unfair to all of society.

As much as we fight about taxation, I feel that the United States has achieved a pretty good balance. We survive as a nation - we bounce back and forth between liberalism and conservatism. Somehow "We the People" make it work in spite of our wacko politicians and their penchant for wars and a multitude of other stupid and pork barrel expenditures. We make some pretty poor choices in our leaders, but our nation is strong enough to withstand their greed, hunger for power, dishonesty, and frequent stupidity. We seem to know, or to have the good fortune, to turn the tables at the proper times. This is undoubtedly the way it will continue to

179

be, and probably the way it should be. We must insist on taxation only with representation and on the ultimate leveling tool – The Vote!

Technology

Dictionary Definition

"Applied science; Technical methods of achieving practical purposes."

Beyond the Dictionary

What a marvelous world we live in! And much of that marvel has been created by technology. Consider, if you will, how your life would be without indoor toilets and plumbing, automobiles, telephones, television, radios, electric lights, the myriad electrical appliances, air flight, space flight, calculators, and computers to name just a few of the things for which we can thank technology.

Life before the things mentioned above had to be more difficult, but please note that I did not say happier. Happiness lies within each individual and does not require material things. Yet the material things, now being existent, become part of the avenue to our current concept of happiness, but I digress.

I speak personally. I would not be alive today if not for the magic of medical technology. I have had Coronary Artery Bypass Grafting and Aortic Valve Replacement. These are technological advances unheard of even the scant 50 years ago when I graduated from Medical School. And there are so many near miraculous advances in all medical fields. How marvelous!

All of the above being said, the other side of the coin must be noted. We have guns, bombs of unimaginable strength, horrible biological weapons, and who can guess what weapons of mass destruction are in the future? Let us hope that wisdom will prevail over evil. And those who pray should do so. However, it will take more than hope or prayer to forestall the potential danger to our world. Any who think and feel should exert every effort within their power to see that strong, level headed, and well motivated leaders be elected to administer our nation's affairs, and this should apply to all nations of the world. I wish I had the answers. I don't, but I will continue to vote conscientiously. It's not hopeless. I feel the good can beat the bad. Watching the wonders of technology and deriving the benefits has been a joy and very likely will continue to be.

Terror

Dictionary Definition

"State of intense fear; Violence committed by individuals or groups in order to intimidate a population or government into granting their demands."

Beyond the Dictionary

To live in terror is one of the chief horrors of life; to commit acts of terror is one of the most horrible things a person or persons can do. How such acts can be committed in the name of a god is a mystery to me, but seems to be accepted, condoned, and encouraged by some so-called religious leaders.

These people seem to be given to the idea that terrorism is the route to achieving their religious and political agendas, and without a twinge of conscience, they order the plundering, mutilation, torture, and killing of those in opposition, and even of neutral position, to them. They even hold valueless the lives of those who share their beliefs or their own lives in order to terrorize. They claim to be civilized, but the very basis of civilization should be preservation, not destruction! I, as I am sure all truly civilized people do, DAMN THEM! They will surely end up destroying themselves as well as seeing the vast majority of this world's populace turn against them.

I have not addressed the roots of terrorism. Certainly there are some valid complaints that religions, societies, and governments have against one another. Unfortunately, there are those people who gain control of these entities who blow those differences and complaints out of rational proportion. These are the leaders, both political and sacerdotal. In general to become a leader in the upper reaches of government and religion, it is necessary to desire power, to have a stubborn determination, and to be something of a zealot. These people feel a sense of being right, and most often they are not right; they are wrong! But they are powerful and determined. Many are zealots with concern only for a cause and

Ben R. Leonard, M.D.

with no concern for humanity. If only they could open their minds to considerate negotiation with resultant peace! But they can't or won't; so they terrorize!

Then there is God's terror: storms, famine, sickness, pain. Why?

Tyrant

Dictionary Definition

"An absolute ruler unrestrained by law or constitution; A usurper of sovereignty; A ruler who exercises absolute power oppressively and brutally; One resembling such as prior noted in the harsh use of authority or power."

Beyond the Dictionary

The question in my mind is why do tyrants exist. If my presumption is correct, they are made to be evil, not born to be evil. I do not believe tyranny and evil are gene linked, yet it is difficult for the vast majority of us of benign character to imagine anyone raising their offspring to be evil. It happens, not frequently, but it happens and too often with dire consequences.

Tyrants can and do cause great pain, suffering, and at times, catastrophe. Consider some of the Roman emperors, some of our slave traders and owners, Hitler, leaders of the Khmer Rouge, Idi Amin, Milosevic, Kim Chong-il, Bin Laden, and Hussein and sons; and remember the horror, havoc, and suffering these people caused and continue to cause. How could these people have developed into tyrants? What well-springs of terror and evil keep producing these abominations we are hesitant to call human beings?

What drives these devilish creatures to commit such atrocities against humanity? Have they no sense of kindness, of justice, of plain old decency? God, these questions drive me nuts! A sane, reasonable human simply hasn't the mind-set or emotional make-up to answer these questions!

Even though we know many of the crimes against humanity the specific tyrants mentioned above have committed, many of us find it difficult to contemplate them without emotional distress and outrage. Tyrants are not to be taken lightly. They and their atrocities demand serious consideration and action on the part of rational and civilized society.

Ben R. Leonard, M.D.

But what and how? I only wish the question of what to do about them was as easy to answer as to ask. Is war the only answer? My God! I hope not!

Virtue

Dictionary Definition

"Conformity to a moral standard of right."

Beyond the Dictionary

From the moment we are able to see and hear with a hint of comprehension, we begin to learn the difference between right and wrong. Those with bad role models will receive the wrong signals and in most instances will develop the traits of immorality and/or dishonesty. Those with good role models will be inculcated with the traits that lead to an honest and moral life – a life of virtue.

Admittedly, the aforementioned precepts are not written in stone, but generally they hold true, and presuming such, then virtue is a learned quality. Further, virtue is a quality to be greatly desired, virtue is extremely valuable, and virtue is highly honored.

The happiest, most productive lives are those of the virtuous. Virtuous people are giving and charitable. They are healers and helpers. They are diligent and trustworthy. They are deliberate and fair in judgment. They strive to do no harm. They fight evil and support that which is good and right. They tend to love rather than hate.

Not only are the virtuous happy and comfortable within themselves, but also they are honored and admired by their peers. They are loved by the recipients of their kindness and generosity. I can't help but believe that theirs are the souls of everlasting peace and contentment.

The sad fact is that few of us on this earth are completely virtuous. Most of us have our flaws, some more than others but all to a greater or lesser degree. The redeeming element is our conscience. Most of us have the ability to feel remorse or shame and the desire to be forgiven. This ability and desire are virtues that complement our lives and compensate, hopefully in great part, for our misdeeds.

Happily, most of us also have the virtue of forgiveness.

War

Dictionary Definition

"A state of open and declared armed hostile conflict between states, countries, or nations; A struggle between opposing forces."

Beyond the Dictionary

War! How horrible and stupid! Is this a creation of God or man?

Or both? There are those who contend that war is a culling process, one of our ways to keep people from over-running the earth, population control. Really? Is this so?

If it is a creation of God, what is the reason? Why would God create humans only to destroy them? Is the earth a giant chessboard for God's enjoyment? Do we fight and plunder and die at the pleasure of our creator? Is war [along with famine, flood, fire, and storm] God's way of controlling our numbers or His game? It is difficult to imagine, and I'm sure many would accuse me of heresy for such questioning, but I do so in benign ignorance.

Did God, as many assert, give humans a degree of free will to, in part, determine our own fate? This is certainly a possibility, and I would be the last to deny this, again because I simply do not know. Presuming we have the power of determination, and it seems likely we have some degree, then how can we be so very thoughtless and frankly stupid as to take human lives for inadequate and often egregious reasons?

Where is reason when we need it? Where is our ability as communicating human beings to sit across the table from those who oppose us and intelligently, thoughtfully talk? Where is our ability to understand the tragedy in the loss of life? Is it that our leaders have something to gain? Is it that our leaders know that their lives are not in jeopardy? Do they feel or understand the terrible tragedy and suffering attendant to war? I wonder.

Oh, yes, there are times to fight. We must protect our freedom and our safety but only after certain knowledge that these are in absolute jeopardy. Preemptive wars are not good enough! There is too much horror in war to start one! Good God! When will we learn?

Wealth

Dictionary Definition

"Abundance of money, valuable material possessions, or resources."

Beyond the Dictionary

Wealth in the material sense is as described in the dictionary, and let no one tell you otherwise, it is desirable. Yet there are other equally important, probably more important, kinds of wealth which concern the mind, spirit, and body.

Who can honestly say that material wealth is undesirable. Money buys food, clothing, shelter, and many of the things that make "The Good Life." It is true that money does not buy happiness, but it allows us the luxuries to enhance our happiness. As wrong as it may be, money opens doors and allows for a modicum, sometimes more, of prestige.

Money talks! This does not mean that one should do anything for material wealth – honor and honesty are far more valuable.

Having extolled the value of material possessions, I must say that there are things more valuable. The worth of good health is incalculable. Just look around to see the physically afflicted. See the stroke victims, the brain damaged, the bed ridden, the heart diseased, the cancer victims, the maimed, ad infinitum. Those who are free of such affliction are indeed wealthy.

Yet more important than the wealth of good health is the wealth of the mind, the spirit, and ultimately the soul.

It is wonderful to have the ability to communicate, to think and reason, to teach and learn. The brain is a wonderful thing, and wealthy is the person who has the ambition and drive to expand its contents, to strive for knowledge and wisdom. Even wealthier is he or she who gains knowledge and wisdom.

Ben R. Leonard, M.D.

Wealthiest of all is the person who achieves happiness and contentment, the person who has learned kindness and honesty, the person who is at peace with his or her spirit, and the person who feels secure with the future of his or her soul.

Why, Shucks! We can all be wealthy!

Wisdom

Dictionary Definition

"Accumulated philosophic and/ or scientific learning; Knowledge with ability to discern inner qualities and relationships."

Beyond the Dictionary

To a certain degree I disagree with the dictionary definition of wisdom. Knowledge is not wisdom, yet wisdom requires knowledge. I will explain to the best of my ability.

First let me acknowledge that knowledge is a wonderful thing to possess, but wisdom takes knowledge a step further. Knowledge is knowing things; Wisdom is the ability to interpret and utilize knowledge. Wisdom does not come as quickly and as easily. Wisdom comes to the learned who have experience and the ability to assimilate and interpret that experience and knowledge. Unfortunately, not all who have knowledge have the innate ability to be wise.

Wisdom is the almost mystical gift that allows its possessor to interpret the how and why of many aspects of life. The wise can almost predict. The wise can advise, but more often than not, refuse to advise specifically to individuals and rather share their wisdom with a more general community.

The wise ones understand love, hate, all the emotions. They understand success as well as futile endeavor, and more importantly, they understand how to handle success and failure.

To some degree the wise even understand how they are perceived; although, this may be demanding too much of wisdom. Robert Burns wrote, "O wad some power the giftie gie us to see oursels as ithers see us! It wad frae mony a blunder free us." Burns was wise.

Ben R. Leonard, M.D.

Yes, it is unfortunate that we all can't be wise, but the redeeming element is that we can all be happy if we learn to accept our lot in life and to live and let live.

And most important, we must love and be loveable. Perhaps this is the soul of wisdom.

Work

Dictionary Definition

"Activity in which one exerts strength and faculties to do or perform something; A sustained physical or mental effort to overcome obstacles and achieve an objective or result; The labor, task, or duty that affords one his accustomed means of livelihood."

Beyond the Dictionary

There's a song, "Love makes the World Go 'Round." Well, so does work make the world go 'round! It makes the whole world, as well as our little individual worlds, go 'round. Work puts food in our mouths, clothes on our backs, and shelter over our bodies.

Work has so often been portrayed solely as a necessity, and that it is, but it is good for body, soul, and spirit too. Certainly, work pays for our needs, but there is something uplifting about being able to pay our way - something of the essence of the person - almost transcending necessity.

Super lucky are those who enjoy their work, but lucky are those who have work - any kind of work, be it physical or mental. So often we hear people say they hate their job, but in most cases, I feel, they are just being rhetorical - just venting steam. Let them lose their job, their work, and then listen to the steam!

Lucky, and with it all, happy are those who work.

There is something to be said for the physical effects of work. Most work, even the mental variety, is good for one's health. It allows for a certain peace of mind which in turn creates a better atmosphere for good physical health. Admittedly, there are jobs that can adversely affect health - working in a coal mine, etc., but hopefully, the unhealthy jobs are on the wane, and we can anticipate generally healthier work environments.

Ben R. Leonard, M.D.

A little advice: If you think you're working too hard, think about the family you are supporting and how wonderful they make your life. If you think you're working too hard, think about the poor and the hungry. Think about how really lucky you are to have work.

Youth

Dictionary Definition

"Period of time between childhood and maturity; The early period of existence, growth or development."

Beyond the Dictionary

What a wonderful vibrant time of life is youth! We're in what I like to call our "Sponge Phase." It's a time when we grow physically, mentally, and emotionally. - we soak up everything around us like a sponge. It's our time to prepare for the future and yet a time for revelry and excitement.

Surprisingly, most of us don't realize the importance of this training and learning period. We become much, possibly too much, taken with the excitement of living and simply having fun. Yet, paradoxically, we are impatient to mature - to get on with our forthcoming adulthood.

The brightest and most ambitious among us tend to devote a bit more time and energy to the preparation aspect. They become the leaders, the scientists, the bosses, the achievers. One might say they are the "Smart Guys," but we can't discount the "Plain 'ol Good Guys" because they bring to life the plans of the "Smart Guys," and they serve in the myriad ways that make our lives more livable. So we are all, in our own way, the "Important Guys." All a product of our youth!

I can't remember who said, "Youth is wasted on the young." As a senior citizen of 76 years with my share of infirmities, I can sympathize with this sentiment recognizing my elder weaknesses, but I really wouldn't have it any other way than the way it is. I remember my youth as a wondrous, exciting time of intense activity and learning, and I loved almost every moment of it, but I also remember the moments of longing and frustration. We only need one such phase in living, then it becomes time to produce, then it becomes time to contemplate, then we finally leave to make way for the young. This is as it should be.

I'm happy for our youth and happy that I had the same experience, but once was enough. Youth is for the young!

Zealot

Dictionary Definition

"A person who has an eager and ardent interest in pursuit of something; A fanatical partisan."

Beyond the Dictionary

Probably more good and more harm have been accomplished by zealots than by any other type of person. Personally, I feel that the world is a worse place because of zealots.

In spite of the good that many humanitarian zealots do, they often end up alienating many with their fanaticism with the result that their cause is damaged. In short, they can be a pain in the ass! Too bad, but true. Fanaticism is rarely rational, and most people prefer a calm, rational approach to life's problems and projects.

The seriously harmful zealots are those who espouse hateful, dangerous, greedy or angry causes. We can name a few: The Christian Crusaders, The Religious Inquisitors, Hitler and the Nazis, some of the Roman Emperors, Stalin, Joseph McCarthy, Saddam Hussein, Arafat, and many more from antiquity to the present. These people and their cohorts have caused incalculable damage to our world – they were and are zealots!

Too often we associate zealotry with religion only. Certainly, the religious zealots of the world deserve their share of the discredit, but we cannot forget the political, sociopathic, and dictatorial zealots who have wreaked havoc.

I look upon zealotry as an illness. It is a disease with no simple cure. In the most severe instances, destruction of the zealot is the only cure. However, perhaps prevention is the best approach. How? We as a world community must be alert. We must try to elect leaders who are honest, intelligent, and alert. This is a big and difficult order because people endowed with these character traits rarely find politics desirable, yet we must try. Last and certainly not least, we must try to stay informed. With our biased media this will be difficult, but again we must try. There will always be zealots, but let's kick 'em in the pants at every opportunity!

And we finish with a little poem:

Words are strange and funny things.

They live on wings,

And they fly and of the wind they are.

And good?

They must not stay

for too oft they hurt.

And pain is worse than joy is good?

Words! Oh, Let them stay!

For if they would away,

Too oft they carry

Love,

And Life,

And the Soul.

Words: Beyond the Dictionary

About the Author

Ben Reese Leonard was born in Tampa, Florida on Feb.2, 1927 of Daniel Benjamin and Ethyl Reese Leonard. After only a few months he was taken to Texas, finally residing in San Antonio from the age of 2 until he finished Brackenridge High School.

At age 18 he entered the U.S.Navy and served as a Hospital Corpsman until the end of World War II being discharged in time to enter the Fall Session, 1946, at the University of Texas in Austin. After 3 years, he was admitted to the University of Texas Medical Branch in Galveston receiving his Medical Degree 4 years later in 1953. He interned at SP General Hospital in San Francisco, California; then served a short residency in urology in Houston, Texas.

Uncomfortable in the specialty of urology, Dr. Leonard found a position with a General Practice Group in the Gustine/Newman Area of California in the San Joaquin Valley. He established his residence and practice in Gustine in October 1954 where he has remained, now going into his 50th year. His practice has involved general medicine, general surgery, obstetrics, and pediatrics. At this time he limits practice to general medicine, pediatrics, and minor surgery. He does not plan to retire.

Dr. Leonard has been active in local and county school boards, Rotary Club serving a year as president, local hospital chief of staff, chairman of the Gustine Diamond Jubilee Committee, chairman and board member of the Gustine Citizens for the 4th of July Committee for more years than he can remember, Gustine High School Football Team doctor for 23 years, National Ski Patrol, and an active participant in numerous community projects.

He is particularly proud of his family. He has been married to his present wife, Arlene, for 26 years. He has 1 daughter, 3 sons, 2 step- daughters and 9 grandchildren. He notes with special pride that all his children are honest, active, and self-sustaining.

Next to his love for family, friends, and his dog, Gypsy, Dr. Leonard loves the mountains and their peaceful grandeur and majesty.

www.ingramcontent.com/pod-product-compliance
Lightning Source LLC
Chambersburg PA
CBHW030314290526
45785CB00001B/350